RIVERSIDE COMMUNITY COLLEGE
1916

ARAB-ISRAEL

P9-AGG-718

AG 18 '94		
AG 2 00		
JA 29 02		
AP 16 07		

DEMCO 38-296

THE ARAB-ISRAELI
SEARCH FOR PEACE

≣IGCC

*A project of the University of California
Institute on Global Conflict and Cooperation*

THE ARAB-ISRAELI SEARCH FOR PEACE

EDITED BY
STEVEN L. SPIEGEL

LYNNE RIENNER PUBLISHERS ▪ BOULDER & LONDON

Riverside Community College
Library
4800 Magnolia Avenue
Riverside, California 92506

MAR 94

Published in the United States of America in 1992 by
Lynne Rienner Publishers, Inc.
1800 30th Street, Boulder, Colorado 80301

and in the United Kingdom by
Lynne Rienner Publishers, Inc.
3 Henrietta Street, Covent Garden, London WC2E 8LU

©1992 by the Regents of the University of California. All rights reserved

Library of Congress Cataloging-in-Publication Data
The Arab-Israeli search for peace / edited by Steven L. Spiegel.
    p. cm.
   Includes bibliographical references and index.
   ISBN 1-55587-313-8 (pb)
    1. Jewish-Arab relations—1973–.   2. Israel-Arab conflicts.
  3. Conflict management—Middle East.   4. Arms control—Middle East.
I. Spiegel, Steven L.
DS119.7.A6727   1992
956.04—dc20   92-19864
                                        CIP

British Cataloguing in Publication Data
A Cataloguing in Publication record for this book
is available from the British Library.

Printed and bound in the United States of America

The paper used in this publication meets the requirements
of the American National Standard for Permanence of
Paper for Printed Library Materials Z39.48-1984.

Contents

Preface

This book, which contains contributions from several continents and countries and diverse political cultures and environments, could not have been accomplished without the assistance and support of the Institute on Global Conflict and Cooperation (IGCC) of the University of California, a unique program that combines the resources of all nine campuses of the University of California in an effort to pursue research on means of controlling international hostilities and promoting cross-country collaboration. The book is one outcome of IGCC's efforts to pursue innovative approaches to existing security problems, including sponsoring programs that bring together scholars and analysts from various countries to analyze a particular, and pressing, issue. The editor and contributors deeply appreciate the efforts of Dr. Susan Shirk, director of IGCC, and Sue Greer and Patty Paterek, of IGCC's staff, in the process leading to publication.

The editor would also like to thank the Center of International Relations (CIR) of the University of California, Los Angeles, for its assistance in the preparation of the book. Dr. Michael Intriligator, former director of CIR, took an active interest in the formulation of the book, and Gerri Harrington, CIR's administrator, played a crucial role in its organization.

A volume this complex would not be possible without the financial assistance of a number of organizations, and the editor thanks the W. Alton Jones Foundation, Inc., the Carnegie Corporation of New York, the Ploughshares Fund, the Canadian Institute for International Peace and Security, the United States Institute for Peace, Mr. Stanley Sheinbaum, and Mr. Albert Friedman.

A variety of student assistants were invaluable in the preparation of this book. They include Alan Kessler, Robin Hardy, and Morgan Tookey. David Pervin was critical in assisting in editing and compiling the manuscript.

—*S.L.S.*

1

Introduction: The Search for Arab-Israeli Peace After the Cold War

STEVEN L. SPIEGEL
DAVID J. PERVIN

FACTORS BEHIND THE PEACE PROCESS

Since the first signs of the Soviet Union's decline, international politics have been undergoing fundamental changes, changes dramatically accelerated in the wake of the breakup of the USSR. In the Cold War era, a relative certainty was generated by the paradox of the superpowers' primacy contrasting with their immobility in the face of competing moves and the threat that miscalculation could lead to global annihilation. With the demise of the Soviet Union, one of the poles underpinning stability has been removed. Particularly apt is Winston Churchill's observation that "I cannot forecast to you the action of Russia. It is a riddle wrapped up in a mystery inside an enigma." Given the great uncertainty as to what roles the United States, the European countries, Japan, and the successor states of the USSR will play in the new international politics, prognostication has become much more challenging. It is far from clear whether there will indeed be a "new world order," as President Bush once promised.

So far the evidence is mixed. Fragmentation and escalating violence in Africa, South Asia, Yugoslavia, and the former Soviet Union contrast with movement toward integration in Europe and conflict resolution in Southeast Asia, Latin America, and South Africa. The abiding question becomes how to accentuate the positive while ameliorating, if not eliminating, the negative tendencies. If a new world order—more tranquil and prosperous— does evolve, it will be the result not only of changes in local balances of power, but also, and mainly, of the conscious and active efforts of leaders, analysts, and engaged activists.

The Middle East has not been immune to the contrasting tendencies of violence and conflict resolution that have thus far characterized the post–Cold War period. Iraq's invasion of Kuwait served as a profound reminder that the use of force remains an ever present option in this turbulent region. Iraq's defeat by the U.S.-led UN coalition was a form of conflict resolution—albeit one that was bloody and had unforeseen ramifications, including the rebellion of the Kurds and Shiites in Iraq. Another, and more promising, form of conflict amelioration began in Madrid in October 1991, where a political negotiating process between Israel and its Arab neighbors contains the potential for producing a viable settlement. If some form of peaceful resolution is to be achieved between these longtime antagonists, it will only be as a result of continuous engagement by all sides.

There are sure to be pitfalls, controversies, and accusations in what is expected to be a prolonged negotiating process. The contributors to this book both outline the possible roadblocks to peace and suggest methods to either bypass or build bridges over them. One recurrent theme of these essays is that the threat or use of force does not solve problems and frequently exacerbates those already existing while generating new ones. The recognition that the resort to military instrument is unlikely to resolve the Arab-Israeli conflict may be one of the factors that helps explain the peace process, unprecedented in scope, that began in Madrid in 1991. Equally important, however, is the end of the Cold War, itself the result of the decline and then rapid demise of the Soviet Union. The Soviet withdrawal from the region has denied radical regimes, such as Syria, their superpower patron and increased the influence of the United States. Indeed, if Saddam Hussein's statements are to be taken at face value, one of the motivations of his invasion of Kuwait was to offset the perceived development of U.S. hegemony in the region, which he feared would be used by Israel for its own purposes. Instead, the Gulf War only enhanced U.S. prestige and influence in the Middle East.

It is clear that the collapse of the Soviet Union contributed to the decision of the various Arab states to participate in the peace process. This reason is emphasized by Ziad Abu-Amr, who argues in his essay that after the Cold War and especially the Gulf War, the "balance of power has further tilted in favor of Israel." M. Z. Diab's analysis of Syrian strategy suggests that the loss of Soviet support, the increased prestige of the United States, and the perception of a stronger Israel led the Arab states to believe that the changed conditions necessitated a new strategy of cooperating with Washington, in the hope that this would lead to greater distance between the United States and Israel. Such a strategy showed early signs of success in the extended debate in early 1992 over linking the $10 billion in loan guarantees to Israel's settlement policy in the West Bank. While the U.S.-Israeli relationship was showing strains before Iraq invaded Kuwait, one of the ironies of U.S. success in the Gulf War is that it raised questions about Israel's strategic value. Thus, contrary to Saddam Hussein's fears of a closer U.S.-Israeli relationship, the end of the Cold

War may have in any case led to greater tension between Washington and Jerusalem.

Other factors contributed to the willingness of the Arab states to engage in the peace process, including severe economic problems in Jordan, Syria, and the West Bank and Gaza Strip, a feeling of obligation to the United States on the part of the Gulf monarchies, and the continuing fear that further conflict might directly threaten domestic stability. As several contributors note, of all the participants, the Palestinians are especially interested in the peace process, both because their straits are the most desperate and because they have the most to gain. The extensive immigration of Soviet Jews to Israel has also led many Arabs to believe that in the future Israel will be even less likely to accept territorial compromise on the West Bank and Gaza, thus increasing the pressure to negotiate now.

The end of the Cold War and the Gulf War also affected Israel in contradictory ways. On the one hand, external threats decreased due to the removal of Soviet support for Israel's most vehement opponents, especially Syria, and the destruction of much of Iraq's military capabilities. The massive immigration of Soviet Jews raised the potential of an economically and militarily more powerful Israel and was seen by some in Israel as increasing the importance of keeping the West Bank and Gaza. On the other hand, the collapse of the Soviet Union could eventually lead to decreased U.S. support for Israel, and the Scud attacks on the Tel Aviv area during the Gulf War brought home the dangers of continued conflict and the limited use of territory for defense in the age of missiles. The influx of Soviet Jews exacerbated preexisting economic problems, making Israel more susceptible to U.S. pressure, and raised questions about the wisdom of spending money on West Bank settlements given the pressing needs of absorption. Indeed, the victory of the Labor Party in the June 1992 elections can in part be explained by its call for the elimination of government subsidies to settlements and the shift of resources to immigrant absorption. In turn, Labor's victory boded well for improved relations with the United States.

The end of the Cold War and the Gulf War has encouraged participation in the peace process by the regional parties. It has also enhanced the position of the United States. With the decline of the Soviet Union, Washington is not merely the most important external actor, arguably the case since 1973, but the *only* one with the potential of exerting effective, if not determining, influence on the course of the peace process. The euphoria that followed the Gulf War, with pundits declaring the world unipolar and pronouncing a U.S. moment, made it seem inevitable that a *pax Americana* had arrived, an "American century" as Henry Luce had put it in an earlier era of hope and anticipation.

Yet, events since have tempered such expectations. Even though the United States is the only superpower, U.S. capabilities to influence events remain limited. As the American public turned inward to deal with the fallout from the end of the Cold War and the domestic recession, the willingness to attempt to exert influence in foreign affairs decreased. There was even talk of a swing of the pendulum back toward isolationism. The contrast between President Bush's 1991 and 1992 State of the Union messages perhaps demonstrates best the changing mood and direction of U.S. politics: in 1991 he was as confident and outward-looking as he was uncertain and inward-looking in 1992. Another symptom of the changing U.S. perspective was the almost complete absence of debate concerning foreign policy in the 1992 presidential primaries.

The limited withdrawal of the United States may offer opportunities for other states to play a larger role in the Mideast peace process. The fact that both European states and Japan attended the multilateral negotiations held in Moscow in January 1992 indicated the possibility of their intensified engagement. That the successor states of the former USSR cannot play a role in the peace process is obvious. Indeed, this inability was already apparent at Madrid, where President Gorbachev's opening speech skirted past the Middle East and consisted mainly of pleas for assistance for the USSR. The impression of disappearing Soviet influence was reinforced at the multilateral meetings, symbolically held in Moscow but paid for by Saudi Arabia. As to the Western European states, they are in the midst of readjusting to their new environment. Their priorities naturally emphasize the threat of destabilization and chaos among their neighbors to the immediate east. The role of Japan is potentially important, mainly as the source of inducements in the form of economic aid and investment, but Tokyo remains unsure of its place in the new world even as it has become engaged in hosting one part of the multilateral talks.

The general retrenchment of external powers is likely to greatly reduce the amount of outside influence to which the Middle East traditionally has been exposed. This may not be such a bad thing, as left to their own devices and no longer able to draw on external sources of power, the regional states may realize that continued conflict is too costly. As Secretary of State Baker has repeatedly emphasized, it is the Arabs and Israelis who will have to live together. Outside parties cannot want peace more than those who live in the region. External powers, especially the United States, still have an important role to play in creating conditions leading to a peaceful resolution of the Arab-Israeli dispute, but that role is limited.

The focus of the essays in this volume is the examination of the contributions that can be made by the regional parties and outside actors to create conditions favoring peace in the Middle East. The book has been divided by substantive areas, beginning with an examination of the factors leading up to the peace process and the importance of properly structured negotiations in facilitating successful conflict resolution. The second part turns to the possible contribution of economic cooperation in sustaining a settlement. The final section explores the issue of arms control, for only when the states feel secure will there be a genuine chance of sustained accommodation. The separation is, of course, merely an analytic device; in reality, all of these factors are deeply intertwined. The role that each can play in reinforcing the others is the underlying theme of this book and one implicit in all of its chapters.

Although outsiders, primarily Americans, have contributed to the essays that follow, the unique quality of those essays can be found in the examples they offer of Arabs and Israelis struggling for means of achieving some form of accommodation in the post–Cold War era. As the reader will undoubtedly agree, the fact that all of the contributors are speaking a similar "language," in terms of concerns and suggestions, is encouraging. They all focus on political stability, economic development, and national and regional security. The reciprocal interaction among these factors has the potential of leading to a spiral upward to peace, but it can also lead downward to renewed warfare. The suggestions of the authors focus on recognizing the relationships among these factors and developing policies that will ensure progress toward conflict resolution. These recommendations are offered in the context of the post–Cold War world, which has created conditions of uncertainty and contradictory movements toward both animosity and accommodation.

FACTORS LEADING TO THE PEACE PROCESS

The decline and demise of the Soviet Union was a historic event marking the end of an epoch. The effects of its disintegration were and are profound. They continue to reverberate throughout the international system, and their future effect is uncertain. As regards the Middle East, the immediate impact was to eliminate the patron of Arab radicalism, arguably eliminating the option of war against Israel. The demise of the Soviet Union not only increased U.S. influence in the region, but also may have made the Arab states more open to the peace process.

As an indication of the new era, in Part I Arab and Israeli analysts assess the forces that led to, and the perceptions of, the peace process. In Chapter 2, Shlomo Gazit argues that the underlying forces leading to instability in the region remain, notwithstanding the events of the past few years. The basic problems in the region have little to do with Israel, but are "directly related to the phenomenon of instability, which is characteristic of Arab countries and society." He notes that in the aftermath of the Gulf War the need to attain a balance of power in the Gulf, decrease internal threats to various regimes, and redistribute wealth to moderate the antagonism between the "haves and have-nots" remains pressing. While the full implications of the Gulf War have yet to be worked out, Gazit points to two that operate to Israel's advantage. First, since Iraq is no longer a threat, the Arabs have no real military option. Second, the demonstrated effectiveness of precision guided munitions (PGMs) relatively benefits Israel's high-tech military. The Arab states have thus warily entered the peace process, fearing that one future implication of the Gulf War is intensified domestic instability and the threat of Islamic Fundamentalism.

As Ziad Abu-Amr notes, the Palestinians have entered the peace process with, if not enthusiasm, at least the recognition of their "dire need of a resolution to the conflict" in order to ameliorate their "suffering under Israeli military rule." This imperative accounts for the Palestinians' willingness to compromise on hitherto fundamental positions concerning the role of the Palestine Liberation Organization (PLO), the inclusion of Palestinians from Jerusalem and outside the occupied territories, and a halt on Israeli settlement building. Abu-Amr argues that preexisting divisions among the Palestinians have been exacerbated by these compromises and that the absence of reciprocal Israeli concessions may "undermine the legitimacy of the Palestinian negotiators" and endanger the peace process. While the peace process has the potential of generating "shifts in positions," these can be either positive or negative. Outside mediators, especially the United States, have a responsibility to ensure success. The alternative, according to Abu-Amr, is the possibility of an "escalation of tension and violence" that would threaten "regional peace, security, and cooperation."

It has often been said that there are many similarities between the Palestinians and Israelis, and the chapters by Shibley Telhami and Galia Golan both emphasize the current sharp divisions within Israeli politics that mirror those among the Palestinians. In the wake of numerous interviews with Israeli politicians and analysts, Telhami suggests that recent international events have reinforced extant positions and strategies. The resilience of these predispositions and divisions in the face of international changes accounts, Telhami argues, for the "political paralysis" that has characterized Israeli politics. Nevertheless, the apparent willingness of the Arabs to consider peace, the economic costs of absorbing the immigrants, the question of how these immigrants will vote in the elections, and the possibility that Israeli Arabs will play an increasing political role have all generated some fluidity, or at least uncertainty, in the direction Israel will take.

Golan also points to many of the same factors underlying the unwillingness of the Shamir government to make any decisions until forced to do so by events. As she notes, there is an increasing recognition in Israel that trade-offs will indeed have to be made between various goals. Pithily profound is her observation that "Israel was faced with the choice between *klita* (absorption—of immigrants) or *shlita* (control—over the territories)." She also demonstrates that a paradox exists when the positions of the Likud and the public are contrasted: while the Likud is not willing to make a deal on the West Bank for ideological reasons but is open to compromise concerning the Golan Heights, the Israeli public's concern for security leads to some willingness to compromise on the West Bank but great reluctance to give up any of the Heights. That the Labor Party seeks to gain an advantage from this paradox by taking a hard-line stance on the Heights further complicates an already complex situation.

The underlying theme of each of these chapters is that the prospects for a successful peace process are limited. As Golan makes clear, there is no real trust among the parties, limited understanding or sympathy for the "other," and perhaps not even a "positive will" to make peace. The current peace process, she argues, is instead the "result of the exigencies of a situation in which the adversaries decide not that they do not want to continue the battle, but that they cannot continue."

I. William Zartman is similarly cautious about the prospects of the peace process, arguing that a "ripe moment," which includes a stalemate damaging to all sides, does not currently exist. He emphasizes the potential utility of "carrots" and "sticks" held by both regional and external actors, including Jewish, Arab, and Christian communities in the United States, in making clear the benefits of accommodation and the costs of deterioration. Regarding the West Bank, he suggests that there is a need to go beyond conventional conceptions of statehood and calls for "imaginative solutions" that involve "new and looser applications of sovereignty."

Although the conditions for peace may not currently exist, the underlying premise of the peace process, as U.S. officials repeatedly emphasize, is that sustained negotiations will lead to changes in the perceptions, attitudes, and positions of the parties involved, both on the official level and in terms of domestic public opinion. How the process is structured is itself significant, as is emphasized by John Marks. Marks draws on the experience of the Conference on Security and Cooperation in Europe (CSCE) to demonstrate that the format of negotiations can affect their outcome. While recognizing the vast differences between the situation in Europe when CSCE began in the mid-1970s and that in the Middle East, Marks suggests that the CSCE's wide scope, flexibility, provisional nature of agreements, extensive participation, and opportunity for trade-offs between issues may serve as a workable model for the Arab-Israeli peace process. He argues that the "Middle East needs and would greatly benefit from a regionwide, cooperative process—a process that makes use of innovative methodology and negotiating techniques to find fresh ways to frame issues." Marks also emphasizes the potential for parallel unofficial interchanges to reinforce the official negotiations.

The six chapters in Part I examine the factors that have led each of the parties to appear at the first direct negotiations between Israel and each of its neighbors—no mean achievement. That there has not been immediate agreement and that recriminations continue to be traded was to be expected, but that the process continues and has become more serious and substantive is encouraging. As Marks notes, in Europe, where the divisions were not as fundamental, the negotiations continued for more than fifteen years, with successes and setbacks all along the way. A process similar to CSCE began in Moscow, where an unprecedented regionwide meeting sought to begin dealing with regional issues, including arms control, the environment, water use, and economic development. In Part II we turn to the potential for economic cooperation to reinforce both the peace process and, hopefully, peace itself.

THE POTENTIAL FOR ECONOMIC COOPERATION

Among the many changes resulting from the demise of the Soviet Union is the increased emphasis placed on economics, both as a source of instability and as a potential realm for cooperation. There is evidence of increased cooperation—with Europe in the lead, closely followed by the U.S.-Canadian Free Trade Agreement and similar arrangements in different regions. Within the Middle East itself, discussion of the usefulness of greater economic cooperation has begun. The region is marked by different resource and factor endowments and thus has the potential for cooperation that would facilitate extensive growth and development. Cooperation would benefit all sides, but in relative terms the poorer states would benefit most. In the past, however, cooperation has been limited by political impediments, a phenomenon obvious in the hostile relationship between Israel and the Arabs, but also critical in inter-Arab relations.

The authors in Part II examine the potential benefits of intensified interchange. Patrick Clawson begins with a general overview of the economies of the Levant countries and Egypt. He argues that although there is significant room and benefits from increased cooperation, in the final analysis politics determines economics. Noting the generally disappointing level of cooperation between Israel and Egypt, he cautions that there are ideological, cultural, and bureaucratic barriers to increased trade and other forms of economic interaction even in the event of regional peace. Nevertheless, he identifies areas of potential immediate and postpeace cooperation that can be implemented to the benefit of all sides; these include water and energy, trade, and capital flows. Given the general absence of capital in the region, with the limited exception of the Gulf countries, a central point is that "the simple reality is that both a better business climate and less perceived instability are necessary conditions for more investment; neither by itself is sufficient." He points out that the United States and the USSR's successor states have an important role to play in creating a favorable environment for economic development.

Although Gideon Fishelson notes that increased economic relations may "help the peace process along," he focuses more on the benefits of cooperation in the wake of peace, including the potential that "economic relations might make formal peace more stable." He anticipates that accommodation will provide the private sector with increased opportunities as political risks and interference decrease. The individual economies have considerable complementarity, and he argues that the expansion of markets and the resulting economic development will mean substantial benefits for all sides. The governments in the region also have an important role to play, which includes improving the area's infrastructure and developing methods of cooperatively allocating water. While noting that a relative economic downturn may occur in the immediate aftermath of a peace agreement, Fishelson argues that in the medium and long term, peace will bring substantial benefits in comparison to continued hostilities.

Jawad Anani, like Clawson, argues that while "scoring agreements on the economic side could lubricate the hard-core political negotiation," in the final analysis "agreement on political terms shall dominate the potential success on the economic front." He identifies natural resources, investment, and finance as areas of potentially beneficial cooperation. Anani also adds that the limited amount of water in the region almost compels agreements; limited investment and cooperation in tourism promises substantial benefits; and coordination in banking will assist in improving economic stability. He also suggests that establishment of international institutions, such as a "water clearinghouse" and a Middle East Bank for Reconstruction and Development, will facilitate cooperation and strengthen peace. External parties, such as the United States, Europe, and Japan, can play important roles in these institutions.

The premise underlying any discussion of economics in a region as highly politicized as the Middle East is that the benefits from cooperation will increase the stakes both in the peace process and then in peace itself; that is, the greater the benefits derived from cooperation, the greater the reluctance to forgo them by breaking the links. All of the contributors in Part II emphasize the potential benefits of nonregional involvement, both politically and economically, in developing and then sustaining these ties. But as Clawson notes, external involvement can also impede new links, as "the more aid, the easier to hide behind autarchic barriers and avoid regional cooperation." There are many barriers to coordination, including domestic interests that benefit from protectionism, bureaucracies that increase their control through red tape, and cultural differences. Overarching all of these, however, are the effects of the continued threats of instability and war. Therefore, the possible role of arms control in the region in ameliorating these threats is the focus of Part III of this book.

THE IMPORTANCE OF ARMS CONTROL

As Gideon Fishelson argues in Chapter 9, "the Arab-Israeli conflict did not originate in recognizable economic causes," and as John Marks notes in Chapter 7, a fundamental impediment to peace in the Middle East is the continued questioning not only of borders, but also of the very right of certain states to exist. One may assume that even if a peace agreement is signed, reluctance to accept the legitimacy of the "other" will remain. Peace would thus be formal rather than normal, defined by legal treaties instead of harmonious relations—the U.S. understanding of normality in international relations. Here lies the importance of properly managed arms control, which has the potential not only of eliminating conditions of instability conducive to the use of force, but also, if stability is sustained over time, of leading to a gradual change in attitudes as well. If there is no capability, intentions may change for the better. In addition, early agreements on arms control, broadly defined, may facilitate subsequent agreement in other areas of dispute.

Mark Heller argues in Chapter 11 that the central goal of any arms control regime should be to minimize the offensive capability of the rivals, thereby reducing the threat of crisis instability generated by the perceived need to strike first. He warns that arms control must not be a "technical exercise carried out in a political vacuum" insensitive to the concerns of both sides. For Heller there are important asymmetries—related to differences in geography, economic resources, manpower capabilities, and weapons mixes—that must be taken into account, and balanced, in any attempt to engage in arms control. One of Heller's principal concerns is that a distinction be made between status quo and revisionist states, and nothing should be done that would weaken the former or strengthen the latter. Given that the vast majority of the region's arms are imported, he also argues that outside powers—first and foremost the United States and Soviet successor states, but also European and Third World suppliers—have an obligation not to disturb the regional status quo. Recognizing that selective attempts to limit arms sales may be seen as disadvantageous both to individual arms suppliers and importers, he calls for "an indiscriminate across-the-board embargo" that would give time for the political process to take root.

In Chapter 12 Alan Platt emphasizes that the problem in the Middle East is not one of arms per se but of political differences. Reinforcing Heller's concerns, Platt argues that "certain flows of arms can aggravate tensions in the Middle East and can make conflict more likely." In reviewing the past record of arms supplies, Platt underscores the difficulties inherent in any attempt to stem the flow of weapons. Given the economic benefits of sales and the increasing number of suppliers, coordination of limitations may be increasingly difficult, and the development of indigenous manufacturing may limit the effectiveness of supplier controls. Platt is particularly concerned about the extent and apparent ease of the proliferation of unconventional weapons—chemical, biological, and nuclear—and missile delivery systems. He thus calls for enhanced enforcement of the various multilateral agreements created to stem the flow of such weapons. Platt does not, however, place sole onus on external powers and argues that regional parties not only can, but have engaged in arms control measures. Limitation-of-forces agreements similar to those contained in the first and second Egyptian-Israeli agreements on the disengagement of forces in Sinai in 1974 and 1975 and the Egyptian-Israeli peace treaty of 1979 should be emulated. He shows how efforts to increase transparency, i.e., the ability of each side to observe the other's military activities, would also greatly assist stability in the region.

The deep and reciprocal linkages between the political process and arms control are made succinctly in Chapter 13 by Abdel Monem Said Aly, who argues that "a political settlement guarantees a hospitable climate for deescalating the arms race, while arms control measures create mutual confidence and stabilize a very destabilized situation." Aly notes that in the past, Egypt accepted geographical limitations on its forces, reducing the possibility of surprise attack. Such agreements "established the precedent of asymmetrical balance of forces as one of the means to address Israeli insecurities in exchange for territories." He extends the principle further to include the possibility of the gradual reduction in nuclear and other unconventional weapons in exchange for military and political agreements, with the ultimate aim being the elimination of such weapons "once full normalization of relations and different types of economic and functional cooperation are installed."

By contrast, M. Z. Diab reminds us in Chapter 14 of the complex forces—historical, ideological, political, and technological—that stand in the way of arms control agreements, much less a full-scale Arab-Israeli settlement. Yet, he argues that since 1967 the Arabs have accepted Israel's reality while fearing expansionism; the central question is thus "What type of Israel?" He notes that as Syria has sought to adapt to the changing international system, in particular the loss of its Soviet patron, it has short- and long-term objectives and strategies relating to Israel and the United States. Diab outlines possible policies that will reinforce the political process by reducing the fear of attack. He also points out that the question of balancing asymmetric capabilities and concerns applies not only to the

Israeli side, but also to the Arab side. The Arabs are worried about Israeli capabilities, including nuclear, but also have security concerns regarding both Arab and non-Arab neighbors. The aim of any arms control measures, especially limitation of exports by suppliers, should be to enhance mutual deterrence and the defensive, rather than offensive, capabilities of regional states.

In Chapter 15, in examining how the lessons from Europe's experience with arms control can be applied to the Middle East, Harald Müller calls for increased transparency, including mutual inspections. Müller notes that among the factors making European arms control successful were the strong role of the United States, the severe threat of the USSR, and mutual recognition, much of which are missing in the Middle East.

The closed and secretive nature of regimes impedes arms control efforts, and thus Müller argues that arms control must be accompanied by a process of "internal democratization." Yet, even if all of these conditions may not exist in the Middle East, he claims that European states and agencies can play a positive role. They can create an environment favorable to regional arms control in a number of ways, including holding seminars attended by Arab and Israeli officials, having representatives participate in inspections, controlling arms exports, and applying pressure—economic and political—on regional parties to reach an arms control agreement. At the very least, Müller cautions that the European states should not do anything that makes the situation worse.

As Diab notes in his essay, Middle Eastern states "still regard the threat and use of force as a legitimate means to protect their vital interests." Changing this perception to one in which force is not seen as an option in settling differences will not be easy. The process of evolving new political attitudes will be prolonged and marked by successes and failures. The role of arms control should be to create an environment in which the political process of recognition, negotiation, and agreement can take place without being threatened, accidentally or intentionally, by the threat or use of force. As the authors in Part III all emphasize, arms control should be broadly defined to include confidence-building measures (CBMs), quantitative and qualitative limitations on exports and imports, multilateral negotiations, and the development of international institutions. Preferably in combination but arguably separately, limited tacit or explicit agreement on arms control, broadly defined, may contribute to peaceful relations between Arabs and Israelis.

CONCLUSION

Both because the international system remains in a state of flux and because the peace process continues, no single book can hope to address all aspects of the events that are rapidly unfolding. While regional problems remain profound, the end of the Cold War and the Gulf War signal previously unimaginable opportunities for regional settlement. The concern of the various authors from different countries who have contributed to this book has been to offer guidelines for improving future policies and actions of third parties, both governmental and private, and regional actors on the difficult path to Arab-Israeli peace.

NOTE

The authors thank Alan Kessler for his assistance.

PART I

FACTORS LEADING
TO THE PEACE PROCESS

2

After the Gulf War: The Arab World and the Peace Process

Shlomo Gazit

Four main issues are on the Arab agenda following the Gulf crisis. The main Arab concern has been to stabilize the Arab system, especially in the Gulf area. Although the Iraqi threat has been reduced, the Gulf can still be a source of instability in the future. The immediate problem is to establish a new balanced system of security arrangements combining Arab forces with U.S. backing. There is a need to build a balance of power among: (a) Iraq, which despite its military defeat can still develop a significant potential threat, and neutralizing the Iraqi threat will remain a major problem in the years ahead; (b) Iran, which was strengthened by Iraq's defeat and can project instability into the area, taking into account its radical approach and enhanced military (including nuclear) buildup; and (c) Saudi Arabia and the Gulf emirates, which are the weak head of this triangle. The complexity of the problem was reflected in the controversy among the Gulf War UN coalition members, which has so far prevented any agreement on the components of future security arrangements.

Another central issue on the agenda is the Arab-Israeli peace process. Most Arab governments are eager to use the "new order" atmosphere and the U.S. commitment to move the peace process and to give a new opportunity to the political option. They want to see rapid progress based on Israel returning all occupied territories (including East Jerusalem) for peace.

A third issue of great concern is the internal stability of the various regimes. Some Arab regimes have been facing severe internal pressures, which increased as a direct or indirect outcome of the crisis. The regime in Algiers was the first to collapse; and this is the first time that an Arab regime is being replaced through democratic elections. Next in the line of vulnerability are the regimes of Iraq and Jordan, though neither has come so far under an immediate threat of collapse. While Saddam Hussein is still in

17

power because of the effectiveness of his internal and personal security units, King Hussein is trying to overcome his internal crisis through his renewed close coordination with the Palestinians and his participation in the bilateral talks.

Finally comes the redistribution of Arab wealth, which is an old inter-Arab issue. After years of decline in the economic aid given by the rich oil-producing states to the poor Arab countries, some indications of change came to the surface. Saudi and Kuwaiti dependence during the Gulf crisis on Egyptian and Syrian political and military backing led them to reciprocate with considerable financial aid. It is still doubtful, however, whether this aid reflects a far-reaching change in the approach of the oil states toward the redistribution of their wealth.

THE "LINKAGE" BETWEEN THE CONFLICTS

The Iraqi invasion and takeover of Kuwait had nothing to do with the Arab-Israeli or Palestinian-Israeli conflict. In a way this crisis served as an unexpected support to the Israeli government, which has always found it hard to present its positions to an outside Western world. The Gulf crisis substantiated the Israeli claim that the real problems of the Middle East have very little to do with Israel, nor would the solution of the Arab-Israeli conflict solve the basic problems of the area; these are directly related to the phenomenon of instability, which is characteristic of Arab countries and society. Furthermore, it served the Israeli claim that a political settlement would not remove the threat to Israel's security and its very existence. Kuwait was at peace with Iraq, and Iraq even had very good reasons to show gratitude toward Kuwait for its lavish support of Baghdad during the eight years of the Iraq-Iran war; and yet, this did not prevent Iraq from using brutal force to invade Kuwait and to destroy Kuwait's independent existence.

Another interesting aspect of the Gulf crisis and war was the insistent Iraqi attempt to bring in the Israeli-Arab conflict and to mobilize Arab support by transforming it into an Israeli-Iraqi conflict.

On August 12, 1990, Saddam made his famous "linkage" proposition, when he offered to link the outcome of the Iraqi occupation of Kuwait with the Israeli occupation of the West Bank, the Gaza Strip, and the Golan Heights as well as with the Syrian occupation of Lebanon. He called for "all issues of occupation, or the issues that have been depicted as occupation in the entire region, [to] be resolved in accordance with the same bases, principles and premises."

Saddam's proposition was rejected by all, with the exception of the PLO and the Palestinians.

With the opening of Operation Desert Storm, Iraq tried very hard to force Israel into the war. By launching modified Scud missiles against Israeli civilian population centers, Iraq was counting on Israel's retaliation policy to work. The Iraqi assumption was that once the war escalated into an Iraqi-Israeli war (possibly with an all-out Israeli war with Jordan), the rest of the Arab world would have no choice but to support Iraq.

Cairo, Damascus, and Riyadh understood Israel's perplexity under these circumstances, and they clearly stated that an Israeli military response under these circumstances would not make them depart from the international coalition. It was the first time that Arab countries had to face the dilemma of choosing between their long-standing and basic anti-Israel policy and their particular interests against another Arab nation; and their decision came loud and clear. One may say that in a way some of the major Arab governments were siding with Israel against an Arab brother country.

THE ARAB WORLD IN THE AFTERMATH OF THE WAR

Kuwait has been liberated and the emir has been reinstated, but the problems facing Kuwait are just beginning. We have heard the strong and popular yearnings for a free, more liberal and democratic regime; we were following the immediate reactions of a people that had been undergoing a traumatic experience and was eager to punish those among them that shared the responsibility for their calamity. First on this list were the many Palestinians—the foreign labor force—that collaborated and supported the Iraqi occupying forces. Almost all were forced to flee.

Another outcome of this same crisis was the far more flexible Kuwaiti position toward Israel, including some readiness to participate in the regional conference on the Arab-Israeli conflict as well as to lift the Arab economic boycott on any trading with Israel.

The impact of these anti-Palestinian persecutions does and will probably have its ramifications beyond the immediate Palestinian-Kuwaiti scene; for example, it bears on the overall Palestinian positions facing the peace process. It has substantially increased among the Palestinians the need for an urgent search for a political solution, and no doubt it had an impact on modifying the Jordanian position and explains Amman's readiness to join the process.

We do not know what might be the final impact of the crisis and the war on Saudi Arabia, on Jordan, and on other countries in the region. Arab masses will not easily forgive and forget their leaders' "shameful collaboration with the imperialistic infidels" and the painful blow these leaders inflicted on their great hopes to see redemption through Saddam Hussein. Saddam's "messianic" message was an attempt to offer an answer to the painful feelings of frustration and despair among most Arab societies, and his defeat came as a blow to their own proper expectations. We have been following the results of the free elections in Algeria and the sweeping success in the ballot of the Fundamentalist Islamic movement; one should not be surprised at some additional delayed and strong reactions.

For more than a decade following its peace treaty with Israel, Egypt had been isolated and ostracized. Things had already begun to change before the Gulf crisis, but the crisis reinstated Egypt in its traditional position, at the helm of Arab politics; this was done without any Egyptian concession on its bilateral Egypto-Israeli relations. Nevertheless, Egypt feels that its problem has not yet been completely resolved; it remains where it was fourteen years ago. Israel, together with Egypt, will have to reach political agreements and solve its problems with all its neighbors. It will also have to reach a comprehensive solution that will leave no unresolved issues that may blow up in everyone's face at any moment. If these issues are not resolved, Egypt will have, sooner or later, to make a very difficult choice between its bilateral interests and problems vis-à-vis Israel and its position and relations with its fellow Arabs.

Saudi Arabia, very much like Kuwait, is demonstrating flexibility on the Israeli issue; Riyadh has agreed to participate in the regional peace conference and has demonstrated some readiness to consider a lifting of the boycott.

There may be cause to raise another question. The last fifty years in the Middle East have been characterized by a strong belief in the ultimate success of Pan-Arabism, of Arab unity. The first serious blow to this aspiration came in 1967. Following President Sadat's peace initiative, the Arab world became torn on the one issue that had always served as a common denominator—the conflict with Israel. The Iraqi occupation of Kuwait and the Gulf War that followed literally split the Arab world on an inter-Arab issue. The critical question today is whether these pieces can be brought together again—can one still hope for Arab unity? Has there now been a watershed to Arab unity and the opening of a new era and still unexplored new directions?

THE WAR IS NOT OVER

One cannot separate future developments in the Middle East in general and in Israeli-Arab relations in particular from the ultimate outcome of the Gulf War. Operation Desert Shield was replaced by Desert Storm, then by Desert Sabre, and although the fighting has ceased, the crisis is not over yet. The main question today is still the same: What kind of new order is going to emerge in Iraq?

President Bush and his allies took great risks in stopping short of demanding total Iraqi surrender on the battlefield. Future developments in the region, as well as the future of the Arab-Israeli peace process, will be greatly influenced by the allies' ability to complete the job of defanging—and eventually unseating—Saddam Hussein. As long as this has not been achieved, there are well-grounded fears that one of the most important U.S. war aims will remain unaccomplished.

We know already that Iraq's military casualties were lower than what was initially estimated. The Iraqi war machine proved to be significantly bigger, and what became a major concern was Iraq's nonconventional capability (with special emphasis on its most advanced nuclear programs). While Iraq's efforts to develop nuclear weapons were no doubt crippled, as long as Saddam Hussein is in power he will not give up his goal of achieving full nuclear capability. Nor can we be reassured that all Iraqi Scud missiles (with conventional or chemical warheads) and launchers were destroyed.

For the time being, Iraq is still a major potential military threat to its neighbors as well as to other countries in the region, with Israel at the top of that list. The hope to bring security and stability in the Persian Gulf area cannot be realized as long as Saddam Hussein and his regime remain in power. And the expectations of seeing the last of Saddam personally are still no more than wishful thinking.

Furthermore, from an Israeli point of view, as long as Saddam is in power, the chances that Iraqi forces will join the Syrians on the "Eastern Front" are pretty slim. The removal of Hussein would only increase the direct military threat for Israel. A new regime in Iraq would probably enjoy international and (especially) Arab support, would be allowed to rebuild its armed forces (including, perhaps, its nonconventional ones), and would be expected to participate in a substantial way in any future Arab-Israeli war.

Although it is still too early to say so in definite terms, it is possible that the main lesson other Arab regimes in the area have learned is that it is quite profitable to follow Saddam Hussein's strategy and philosophy of bullying, threatening the use of force (or indeed using it), and taking hostages—all this provided you are careful not to overdo it.

THE MAIN ARAB ACTORS

Saddam did overdo it; the coalition that included important Arab member-states proved to be the victory of the so-called pragmatist bloc, now headed by Egypt and Saudi Arabia. Simultaneously, we saw the weakening of the small and partly isolated Arab radical group. This process was greatly influenced by the decision of Syria and Libya to improve their relations with Egypt and other moderate regimes. The result was the formation of a new Arab coalition, headed by Egypt, Saudi Arabia, and Syria. Both Egypt and Syria played a very important role during the war—they provided inter-Arab legitimization to the U.S. military operations against Iraq.

Egypt emerged from the crisis with considerable gains, both politically and economically. Cairo understands, however, that these gains are very much dependent on advancing the Arab-Israeli peace process. No wonder the Egyptians have assumed an important position in their efforts to bring the parties together, offering various suggestions for surmounting some of the existing obstacles. During the crisis Egypt was furious with the PLO and Jordan; Egypt's pragmatic approach today has led it to reestablish active relations with the two. Egypt realized that without the PLO and Jordan there would be no peace process.

One of Egypt's interesting suggestions was to convince Israel to offer as a peace gesture to freeze completely the establishment of new settlements in exchange for an Arab countergesture that would call off the forty-three-year-old economic boycott of Israeli goods and of all foreign firms that trade with Israel. It is interesting to note that while Israel rejected this offer, there were no open voices of dissent or criticism from any of the Arab parties.

The political changes in the Middle East since the end of the war (the survival of Saddam, the diminishing posture of the United States in general and of President Bush in particular, and the major international problems that have eclipsed the political importance of the Middle East and the Arab-Israeli conflict) have increased Egyptian concern and interest in seeing quick political advance.

Saudi Arabia has learned the lessons of the Gulf crisis. While the Saudis have decided to continue with their various military procurement and buildup programs, their most important lesson was that when facing a true and serious military threat from the outside they would prefer a Western presence to support them.

It was expected that the Saudis would show much more moderation and would make positive gestures toward Israel, as a kind of compensation for the restraint Israel showed during the war and as a way to bring the Shamir government to the peace conference. It was not long before their enthusiasm cooled off and their direct involvement in the preliminary peace negotiations became minimal.

Syria proved to be one of the big winners of the crisis and the war. We know, of course, of the Syrian success in implementing the Taif agreements in Lebanon. We do not know if it was just a Syrian initiative to act quickly in Lebanon while everybody else was busy and preoccupied with Iraq, or if Damascus had some precise indications that Syria had a free hand to go ahead with its plans. The result, however, was the same. It remains to be seen if the *pax Syriana* in Lebanon will indeed be consolidated. For the time being, one should not be overoptimistic.

As to negotiating a peace agreement with Israel, we do not believe that the regime in Damascus has changed its goals or strategy; there is no doubt, however, that the Syrians are trying hard to transmit a pragmatic image, willing to open a new chapter in their relations with the United States and projecting flexibility toward Israel by the positive answer they have given to Secretary Baker on the peace process. The first two phases of the peace talks, in Madrid and in Washington, gave no reason to hope for a quick political breakthrough.

Lebanon too has joined the peace process with an independent delegation. We have seen, however, that the Lebanese delegation is receiving its directives from Damascus.

Jordan could have been one of the major losers during the crisis. Following its close relations with Baghdad (and its economic dependence on Iraq), Jordan was one of the few Arab countries that supported, or at least did not take a resolute stand against, Saddam Hussein. Saddam answered the Jordanians' popular aspirations for a strong Arab leader who would unite the Arabs into a major power, stand up to U.S. power, and force the rich Gulf emirates to share their wealth with the poor Arab states.

In adopting this policy, King Hussein was simply responding to the strong popular pressures in his country. Jordan had to pay a costly price for it in its relations with Washington as well as in the complete stoppage of Arab financial support to Amman.

Another most unwelcome result of the war was the expulsion of hundreds of thousands of Palestinian workers from Kuwait, Iraq, and most other oil-producing countries. Their return to Jordan as refugees created a very serious problem of unemployment.

The end of the war eased the pressure on Jordan. Amman's correct assumption was that with the war over, the new Arab and international interest would prefer the survival and stability of the Hashemite regime to any alternative. Surprisingly, it was Shamir's Israeli government that was advocating to understand the special internal difficulties of Amman and was calling to make a renewed effort to bring Jordan into the peace process. Jerusalem understood that the only way to avoid direct Palestinian representation in the peace conference (with a strong linkage to the PLO in Tunis) was to bring Jordan in. Israel's Likud government made a clear decision to renounce (for the time being, at least) the theory that "Jordan is Palestine."

Jordan's severe problems are not over yet. The regime tried to consolidate its position by moderating the radical atmosphere and by reducing the political power of the Islamic groups that enjoy widespread popular support.

The Palestinians in general took a similar position, though for somewhat different reasons. They were frustrated by the failure of the intifada to produce tangible political results and worried by the widespread Israeli momentum of settlement building in the occupied territories and the massive influx of Jewish immigrants from the USSR. From this point of view, the Palestinians considered Iraq as the only credible challenge to Israel's military superiority and as the potential party capable of uniting the Arabs into a major regional power that could challenge the U.S. hegemony in the Middle East.

The Iraqi missile attacks on the civilian centers of Israel were welcomed enthusiastically by the Palestinians. Many of them were watching the incoming missiles from their rooftops in the West Bank.

This attitude was damaging to the PLO and the Palestinians both politically and financially. The PLO's support of Iraq undermined its relations with both the Arab and Western members of the coalition. In the view of most of the coalition members, the PLO's position as the representative of the Palestinians in the peace process was damaged. The financial aid given by the Gulf states to the Palestinians was considerably reduced, and the Palestinian communities in some of those states were suppressed.

The Palestinians' support of Saddam and their jubilation at the Iraqi missiles launched against Israel also played an important role in the Israeli "peace movement"; it had a sobering effect. Many in Israel were realizing for the first time that when Palestinians were discussing and offering peaceful solutions to the conflict, it was not because of their humanistic and pacifist antiwar feelings. It was because of a clear understanding that this was the only pragmatic and feasible solution available for them. And, of course, this could have important ramifications in future negotiations.

THE FUTURE REGIONAL MILITARY BALANCE

The Gulf War had and will have some important strategic ramifications in the region. One cannot discuss the Arab world after the war nor the Arab positions in face of a possible Arab-Israeli peace process without a brief mention of two of these developments.

First, from an Israeli point of view, stands the Iraqi military defeat and the severe crippling of its military capabilities. The immediate result is that no Arab military coalition can count on a significant Iraqi expeditionary force to join Israel's eastern front. We have no way to know if or when the Iraqis will be able to rebuild their military forces; but if they decide to do so, it will no doubt take them several years. The main implication will be that the Arab parties will probably have to enter the peace process without a feasible alternative military option.

The war itself taught two major military lessons, both of which have had and will have some very important consequences. The first concerns the massive use of precision guided munitions (PGMs). The allied massive use of these weapons clearly showed the incomparable advantage they have over conventional ammunition. But that isn't all: PGMs need a different quality of personnel to manipulate them; with the possible exception of Israel, PGMs create an almost complete dependence on foreign suppliers, with the obvious political strings attached; and PGMs are expensive. The cost of acquiring the necessary numbers of PGMs is too high for Middle Eastern armies, except for the rich oil-producing countries.

The other lesson from the war concerned the introduction of nonconventional weapons into the Middle Eastern theater of operations. This will no doubt have much greater strategic bearing on the future of the region. Although Iraq did not use its chemical weapons during the war, we know that it had the capability. And indeed, from the Israeli point of view, Israel's behavior and reactions during the crisis and the fighting were based on a worst-case assumption, that Iraq might launch at any given moment modified Scud missiles with chemical warheads. Any future war will have to take into account this threat. Furthermore, we know much more today about Iraq's effort to develop an independent nuclear capability, and it was only a question of a year or two before they would have reached this goal. The collapse and disintegration of the Soviet Union have created a new threat— the availability of nuclear devices for sale and smuggling as well as the vast number of scientists and engineers that might be "bought" or hired to join local Arab efforts to develop and produce arsenals of nonconventional weapons. All involved in Arab-Israeli relations will have to view the future existence of nuclear weapons in the Middle East as inevitable, with strategic and political implications on the peace process.

Can one draw an analogy from Soviet-U.S. relations and assume the possibility of a nuclear "balance of terror" in Arab-Israeli relations? Caution is advised for a variety of reasons: Do all parties concerned understand the extreme change that nuclear weapons will introduce into the strategic equation of Arab-Israeli relations? What will be the impact on the political positions and on the need to work hard toward an urgent political solution? This is yet to be seen.

* * *

The end of the Gulf War gave reason to hope that the Middle East will see a real turn in the main trends in the region. At this stage, unfortunately, one cannot say that this has happened or is about to happen in the foreseeable future. What will happen will depend mostly on U.S. policy and initiatives in the area, on the survival of Saddam Hussein and his regime and future Iraqi inter-Arab policies, on the Arab-Israeli peace process and its possible political breakthroughs, and on Syria's future internal and regional policies—especially its continued efforts to achieve independent military parity with Israel.

3

Palestinian-Israeli Negotiations: A Palestinian Perspective

ZIAD ABU-AMR

While the Palestinians are genuine in their search for a peaceful solution to their conflict with Israel, it would be too simplistic to explain their concessionary position in altruistic terms. Both the Palestinians of the occupied territories and the PLO in exile are in dire need of a resolution to the conflict.

The Palestinians of the West Bank and Gaza are very eager to put an end to their suffering under the Israeli military rule. A peaceful solution carries within it a prospect for salvation and the realization of national rights. The Palestinians also hope that participation in the negotiations will result in halting aggressive Jewish settlement activity in Palestinian land. The Palestinians are wary of further Israeli land confiscation to settle successive waves of Soviet Jewish immigrants.

The PLO's flexibility is motivated by the same concerns and considerations of the Palestinians in the occupied territories. Failure to act and deliver would undermine the PLO's internal legitimacy. Furthermore, the PLO has been isolated because of its attitude toward the Gulf War, both on the Arab level and internationally. Endorsing the U.S.-sponsored peace process and sanctioning Palestinian participation in it were bound to break, or at least relax, the state of siege imposed on the PLO. The PLO also feared the exclusion of the Palestinians from a peace settlement if the organization chose to ban Palestinian participation in the negotiations.

Even if it does not expect any real gains from the peace process, the PLO hopes that a constructive and flexible position may help the organization and its leadership rehabilitate themselves with the Arab world and internationally. Palestinian-Egyptian and Palestinian-Syrian reconciliation, following the antagonistic relations during the Gulf crisis, are cases in point.

Finally, Palestinian concessions are motivated by a sense of realism and pragmatism. Both the Palestinians of the occupied territories and the PLO are aware of the existing balance of power, which is clearly not in their favor. This balance of power has further tilted in favor of Israel since the end of the Cold War and, in particular, in the aftermath of the Gulf War.

The credibility and solid influence of the PLO vis-à-vis the occupied territories may have slightly eroded in the past few years, but the PLO remains the only source of legitimacy for Palestinian participation in the peace process. The PLO's position may have been undermined because of the kind of concessions the organization has made or sanctioned in order to ensure Palestinian participation in the peace negotiations.

Lack of national consensus among the Palestinians of the occupied territories regarding participation in the negotiations is another factor for undermining PLO credibility. Certain PLO factions, such as the powerful Popular Front for the Liberation of Palestine (PFLP) and the Palestinian Islamic groups (the Islamic Resistance Movement—Hamas—and the Islamic Jihad), oppose Palestinian participation in the negotiations.

Nationalist opposition rejects the terms of Palestinian participation, while Islamic opposition emanates from doctrinal considerations. But nationalist and Islamic opposition has not gone far enough to impede Palestinian participation in the negotiations. The opposition fears the grave consequences of sabotaging the peace process. It is also not certain that this opposition can stand up to the mainstream faction (Fatah and its allies), which is committed to participation in the negotiations.

Palestinian negotiators have so far been deriving their legitimacy from the PLO patronage. These negotiators do not have independent power bases of their own. It is rather obvious that any Palestinian success in the negotiations would solicit further popular support for the peace process and Palestinian participation in it. Lack of progress is bound to create a reverse effect and strengthen the opposition camp.

STRUCTURE OF THE NEGOTIATIONS

By agreeing to participate in the regional peace conference, the Palestinians gave their endorsement to the U.S.-sponsored two-track approach to negotiating a peaceful settlement of the Arab-Israeli conflict and the Palestinian issue. In order to enable the peace conference to convene, they abandoned their previous insistence on participating in the conference in an independent Palestinian delegation. Instead, they agreed to participate through a joint Palestinian-Jordanian delegation. They also accepted, with strong reluctance, the exclusion from the delegation of representatives from Arab East Jerusalem.

While agreeing to the exclusion of direct PLO participation in the negotiations, the Palestinians warn that a total and permanent exclusion of the PLO may undermine the legitimacy of their participation and cause a collapse of the negotiations. They also feel strongly about the need to have present in the negotiations outside representatives (from the United States, the former USSR, the European Community, and the UN). Those outside parties are expected to play a mediating role if the negotiations are stalemated. They can act as witnesses and arbiters. Outside representatives will also be needed to guarantee any eventual agreement. The UN participation is particularly important from the Palestinian point of view because the UN represents international legitimacy. The UN is the international body that is expected to endorse concluded agreements. Furthermore, because of its permanency, the UN stands to be the most logical sponsor of the negotiations.

VENUE

While Israel insists that bilateral and multilateral negotiations should move to the Middle East immediately after the opening of the peace conference in Madrid, the Palestinians, and for that matter the rest of the Arab participants, insist that negotiations should be held outside the Middle East region.

The Arab side argues that it is still premature to rotate the sites of negotiations among Israel and each Arab country, as Israel suggests, since this act may be construed as an act of normalization. The Palestinians prefer to hold negotiations outside the region because they believe that they cannot negotiate with the Israelis on equal footing while they are in a place that is under the control of the Israeli occupation authority. Under such conditions they may be restricted, harassed, or even jailed. Negotiating under the thumb of occupation is also a psychological handicap. PLO access to the Palestinian negotiators will be restricted and informal contacts with them can be monitored.

It may be possible, however, to conduct negotiations in the Middle East at a later stage, when some progress in the process is already achieved and when the psychological and political climates become more amenable. But in the meantime, perhaps some informal contacts, or even some form of negotiations on the least complicated issues, can take place in the region. Reaching an agreement on minor issues may induce the Palestinians to negotiate in the region. Parallel or alternate negotiations on separate issues can be conducted inside and outside the region simultaneously.

Finally, Palestinians believe that it is common diplomatic practice for adversaries to start negotiations in third-party territory before some progress is achieved and agreement is reached to move the site of the negotiations back to the region and the territories of the respective parties.

All of that having been said, the Palestinians may be amenable to the idea of holding bilateral talks in Cairo. After all, they had agreed in 1989 to hold bilateral talks with the Israelis there under U.S. patronage. And the Israelis may not object to the idea of Cairo as the site for negotiations, since Egypt and Israel recognize each other, have established diplomatic relations, and are bound together by a peace treaty.

AGENDA

An issue critical to the continuation of the negotiation process is agreement on the agenda for bilateral Palestinian-Israeli negotiations. Although there is initial agreement between the two sides on direct negotiations, setting the agenda may create differences and even a dispute. The Palestinians will insist on including East Jerusalem on the agenda, while Israel is expected to reject this demand. If the Palestinians agree to participate in the negotiations without the suspension of Israeli settlement activity as a precondition, they will insist on putting the issue on the agenda. Beyond that, the Palestinians and the Israelis are likely to agree on including most other issues, such as the nature of Palestinian self-rule, the transfer of authority to the Palestinians in the occupied territories, the existing Israeli settlements, the return of refugees, security arrangements, and the final status of the West Bank and the Gaza Strip.

Including these issues on the agenda, in the short, immediate, or long term, together with the issue of Jerusalem, is considered a minimal condition for continued Palestinian participation in the negotiations. As a gesture of flexibility, the Palestinians may accept the inclusion of some of these items on the agenda of the multilateral negotiations instead of the bilateral talks. From the beginning of peace negotiations in Madrid on October 30, 1991, until the beginning of the third round of talks in Washington on February 24, 1992, the Palestinians and the Israelis had not yet agreed on an agenda.

But of course, agreeing on an agenda does not mean that the two sides will necessarily reach agreement on any of these issues. For example, the way the Palestinians interpret self-rule does not coincide with the Israeli understanding of this arrangement. The Palestinians rely on U.S. assurances that self-rule includes Palestinian control over resources, including land, and not simply autonomy for the population. For a start, the Palestinians will insist on returning state land to their autonomous authority.

NEW SETTLEMENT ACTIVITY

While the Palestinians are willing to negotiate the future of existing Israeli settlements in the occupied territories in the course of the negotiation process, they demand the suspension of new settlement activity during this process. According to the Palestinians, the suspension of settlement activity is not only a confidence-building measure, but also an issue of substance. Furthermore, conducting negotiations without the prior suspension of new settlement activity will render these negotiations meaningless.

The Palestinians are reluctant to accept the notion of putting the issue of new settlements aside and directly proceeding to negotiate other issues pertaining to the interim period of self-rule. This notion is alarming because negotiating on the interim period may take a long time, during which Israel will have built more settlements and made the future resolution of the problem of existing settlements more complicated, in addition to undermining the principle of "land for peace" on which the current peace process and negotiations are predicated. Going to the negotiations with such gloomy prospects, and without a suspension of new settlement activity, would undermine the internal legitimacy of the Palestinian leadership. Furthermore, agreeing to a start of the bilateral negotiations without a prior Israeli commitment to the suspension of new settlement activity may make it difficult in the future for the Palestinians to stipulate their continued participation in the negotiations on the fulfillment of this demand.

In spite of Israel's refusal to suspend new settlement activity after three rounds of bilateral Israeli-Palestinian negotiations, the Palestinians continue to participate in the negotiations. But increasing internal Palestinian pressure and objections to negotiations under such circumstances may cause the Palestinians to withdraw from or boycott the negotiations. Palestinian opposition to negotiations while new settlement activity is still taking place argues that no formal agreement with Israel is needed if Palestinian land cannot be protected from further Jewish settlement. If the objective is a measure of self-rule for the population, which boils down to an improvement of life conditions, the Palestinians should not formally concede their historic and legal rights to Israel and transform the Palestinian issue into an internal Israeli concern. Improving life conditions of the Palestinians may be attained by a decision on the part of the Palestinians to "mind their behavior." A conscious act by the Palestinians to stop the intifada and acts of violence may alter the existing relationship between the occupier and the occupied.

A temporary freeze (a period of ninety days, for example) on new settlement activity is bound to encourage the Palestinians to engage in meaningful bilateral negotiations on the interim period. If progress is made by then on issues of substance, including the suspension of settlement activity, then this issue will no longer be an issue. If no agreement is reached, the negotiation process may be suspended until further agreement on the subject is reached.

It is not yet clear how the Palestinians would react, beyond their public posture on new settlement activity, to a compromise proposal of suspending new settlement construction while allowing Israel to expand on some of the existing settlements in a restricted fashion for practical purposes. Finally, the Palestinians hope that the outside participants in the peace conference will pressure Israel to stop new settlement activity. The Palestinians realize that these negotiations involve mediation (mainly by the United States) and mutual compromises (by the Palestinians and the Israelis). And when the negotiations come to a deadlock, the mediator is expected to ask both sides, not just one, to compromise.

Regarding the future of existing settlements, the Palestinians prefer the dismantling of these settlements, or at least the evacuation of Jewish settlers from them. The West Bank and Gaza constitute a small geographic entity. The Palestinians will need every geographic space to rehabilitate hundreds of thousands of refugees living in the occupied territories and the diaspora. Existing Israeli settlements can be used to accommodate Palestinian refugees who choose to return instead of being compensated according to UN Resolution 194.

But, of course, in a context of peace and cooperation, other options regarding the existing Jewish settlements may be considered. The Palestinians may, for example, be willing to accept the presence of some Jewish residents in their entity as long as these residents remain subject to Palestinian jurisdiction, if the absorptive capacity of this entity permits, and, of course, if the principle of reciprocity and mutual trade-offs is accepted by the Palestinian and Israeli sides.

THE INTERIM PERIOD AND THE FINAL STATUS

While the Palestinians have agreed to go to the peace conference to negotiate self-government without linking any agreement on it to agreement on the final status of the Palestinian occupied territories, they will in the course of the negotiations try to link the interim solution agreement to the future final status of the West Bank and Gaza. The primary Palestinian concern in this regard is to make sure that the interim solution will not become a final solution to the Palestinian problem. If the Palestinians cannot get any commitment during the negotiations on the interim period regarding self-determination or statehood, they will try to make sure that their right to determine their future after the end of the interim period will not be prejudiced by the terms of the interim period itself. They will insist that the interim agreement be very explicit and unambiguous on this issue. For this purpose, they will also request guarantees to ensure that their future prospects are not blocked and that they will be able to exercise their right to choose. These guarantees may be incorporated in the interim agreement itself or included in some parallel document that would be recognized by the parties involved.

The specific terms the Palestinians demand could be inspired by public U.S. pronouncements, especially the formula of "land for peace" and the fulfillment of legitimate political rights of the Palestinians; UN Resolutions 242 and 338; the U.S. letters of assurances and invitations to the peace conference; and even the Camp David accords, where they are pertinent. It is obvious that the parties involved, especially the Palestinians and the Israelis, do not agree on one specific document as an ultimate frame of reference for the negotiations as a whole.

If an interim agreement on self-rule is reached between the Israelis and the Palestinians, this agreement will involve a transfer of authority to a Palestinian body, an interim self-government. Elections may become necessary to select the new Palestinian authority, and it is very likely that those elections will be the first practical step in implementing the Israeli-Palestinian agreement. The two parties may, however, agree on a transitional period to create an appropriate political context before proceeding to actual elections.

Before sanctioning elections, the Palestinians are likely to insist on the fulfillment of certain demands. Some of these demands are: (1) the withdrawal of Israeli forces from population centers where elections are to take place; (2) the participation in the elections of the Palestinians of the West Bank, including Jerusalem, and the Gaza Strip, as well as the persons displaced since 1967 and the deportees; (3) the release of Palestinian prisoners and detainees (who number in the thousands); (4) the supervision of the elections by an international body; and (5) the rescinding of all existing orders, regulations, or laws that prohibit and/or restrict assembly, movement, and participation in political activities or campaigning for elections to enable the elections to proceed in an orderly and democratic manner.

NEGOTIATIONS AS A PROCESS

The Palestinians support the notion of making negotiations a continuing process. This notion carries prospects for the Palestinians and the Israelis alike. Once agreement on the interim period is reached, negotiations should continue in order to reach another agreement on the final status. Arriving at an agreement in this sphere at an early stage will be a catalyst for regional normalization and cooperation between Israel and the Arab states. It is unlikely that actual normalization of relations between Israel and its Arab neighbors would take place before agreement is reached between Israel and the Palestinians on the final status of the West Bank and Gaza. Furthermore, agreement between the Palestinians and Israel may affect positively other bilateral relations, especially between Syria and Israel. But the implementation of Palestinian-Israeli agreements may hinge on concluding an agreement between Syria and Israel.

Since the Palestinians have a stake in the negotiations and their outcome, they will be willing to support the notion of prolonging the negotiation process if that becomes necessary to achieve concrete results. But a freeze on new settlement activity will in this case be essential. The Palestinians may also be willing to start negotiations on the least complicated issues and temporarily postpone talks on thorny issues, such as Jerusalem, until the negotiation process becomes irreversible, but also provided that new settlement activity is suspended, and provided that such issues are put on the agenda.

The Palestinians view favorably the idea of parallel negotiations. Parallel informal negotiations may be necessary to keep the peace process going. If formal negotiations are deadlocked, then parallel informal negotiations can act as a catalyst to resume them. Such informal negotiations can explore new ideas and compromises and can function as a testing ground for the formal negotiations.

MUTUAL CONCESSIONS, CONFIDENCE-BUILDING MEASURES, AND TRADE-OFFS

In order to be able to participate in the conference, the Palestinians made a number of concessions, primarily in deference to Israel. To name but a few, the Palestinians agreed to be represented in the conference by a joint Palestinian-Jordanian delegation instead of an independent Palestinian delegation. They also agreed to exclude from the negotiating delegation representatives from East Jerusalem and from the PLO and the Palestinian diaspora. Finally, they agreed to go to the conference without a suspension of Israeli settlement activity, and without tying agreement on the interim period to agreement on the final status. But the Palestinians believe that if the concessions they have made are not reciprocated by Israel, the continuation of the negotiation process may be endangered. One-sided concessions are bound to undermine the legitimacy of the Palestinian negotiators and strengthen the hands of Palestinian political opposition to the conference and the negotiations with Israel.

Confidence-building measures and the creation of mutual trust will be instrumental in the continuation and perhaps the success of negotiations. For example, the Palestinians would like to see a suspension of Israeli settlement activity. Relaxation of Israeli restrictions on the Palestinians in the West Bank and Gaza would act as another confidence-building measure. The Palestinian negotiators should not be harassed, interrogated, or jailed, since such acts may stress the psychological and political climate of negotiations.

Israel has, however, been doing the opposite. Since the peace conference and the negotiations have started, the Israeli authorities in the Palestinian occupied territories have taken a variety of harsh measures, including a military order to deport twelve Palestinians from the West Bank and Gaza. While such measures have not yet spoiled the negotiation process and have not caused a Palestinian withdrawal from the process, continued Israeli harassment is bound to undermine confidence in the whole peace process. If this harassment exceeds tolerable limits, Palestinian negotiators may come under internal pressure to withdraw, since the continuation of a process that cannot even mitigate Israeli harassment, let alone retrieve Palestinian rights, would become self-defeating.

While the Palestinians may be flexible on the time frame of negotiations, acting upon the advice that all negotiation processes are usually lengthy, the failure of Israel to provide the Palestinians with encouraging signs, at least in the form of confidence-building measures, would frustrate the Palestinians, especially when they are very keen to move ahead with the negotiations.

The concept of trade-offs is both a confidence-building measure and a key element for the continuation and success of the negotiations. Although the construction of Israeli settlements in the occupied territories is considered illegal under the Geneva Conventions, and by stopping this construction Israel would only comply with UN resolutions and not make concessions, the Palestinians expect to be asked to reciprocate an Israeli decision to stop new settlement activity. A number of ideas have been circulating in this respect, such as the proposal to link the suspension of new settlement activity to a temporary halt of the intifada, especially while negotiations are taking place. Another idea is to relax Arab trade boycott regulations against Israel.

Since negotiations have their own dynamics and their own logic, shifts in positions are to be expected. These shifts may result in the collapse of the process on one extreme, or, on the other extreme, in breakthroughs leading to unexpected agreements on the most critical issues. These shifts can also affect the entire context of negotiations as well as their content and pace, and induce the two parties to make substantial concessions. But, of course, it is up to the negotiators to make negotiations a success or a failure. The United States, as the primary mediator, carries a special moral and political responsibility and is therefore expected to play an instrumental role to ensure the success of the negotiations and of the peace process as a whole.

CONCLUSION

It is obvious that Palestinian-Israeli negotiations are conducted under a balance of power that is tilting heavily in favor of Israel. As was indicated earlier, the Palestinians have been aware of this fact. The kind of concessions they have made so far, and the degree of flexibility they have demonstrated, reflect this awareness. But focusing on the balance of power as the primary and sole dynamic for negotiations would defeat the purpose of these negotiations. The Palestinians may decide, in the absence of any Israeli reciprocity, that continuing Palestinian participation in the current peace process is counterproductive. An interruption of Palestinian participation in the negotiations may cause the collapse of the whole peace process. This collapse may itself become a factor in the escalation of tension and violence in the occupied territories and the Middle East region and hence impede prospects for regional peace, security, and cooperation.

4

Arab-Israeli Peace Negotiations: An Israeli View

GALIA GOLAN

There are a number of ingredients for success in a negotiating procedure, some of which may be perceived as necessary though not necessarily sufficient, some merely desirable but not absolutely essential. Indeed, in the long and complicated prenegotiation negotiations conducted by U.S. Secretary of State Baker after the close of the Gulf War, many conditions, preconditions, and stipulations were raised by the various parties concerned, to the point that barely any of the necessary ingredients for successful negotiations appeared to be present, or to remain when the Arab-Israeli peace talks finally began in Madrid.

Clearly, a positive ingredient should have been trust or, minimally, some reduction of suspicion on the part of the adversaries. This might have been achieved through confidence-building measures; such measures were sought by the United States for just this purpose. Yet, it proved impossible to obtain confidence-building measures prior to the opening of negotiations precisely because of the overwhelming lack of trust between the parties. These negotiations are clearly between enemies, as is usually the case of negotiations to close a state of belligerency or war. Indeed, these are enemies who have been locked in battle in one form or another for fifty-four years, actually in some ways for over a hundred years.

There have been contacts over the years; there has been a modicum of prenegotiation negotiation and citizen diplomacy. It might even be true that some of this has constituted a learning process that may have contributed to a somewhat better, more sophisticated understanding of the adversary on the part of those involved. Palestinians and Jordanians may have gained both an appreciation of Israelis' fears and an awareness of the varieties of sentiment in Israeli society and body politic; Israelis may have gained an understanding of the complexities of internal Palestinian politics and an appreciation of the

37

desperation experienced by those living in the occupied territories. Certainly, the individuals who actually participated in previous peace negotiations with the Arabs, namely in the Israeli-Egyptian talks of 1977–1979, came away with a greater understanding and belief in the possibility of Arab-Israeli peace. Yet, few of the persons involved then are among today's negotiators, and little of the experience and understanding accrued through these and other contacts has been conveyed to the public in Israel as a whole. Indeed, even the historic peace with Egypt is viewed in Israel as a "cold peace," its significance therefore greatly underestimated by many.

Without belittling the potential value of confidence-building measures, citizen diplomacy, and informal prenegotiation negotiations, it is unrealistic to expect Israel and the Arabs to conduct this peace process with the benefit of trust. A more accurate image would be one of parties still locked in battle, adversaries still at war with one another.

A second ingredient would be a will for peace on the part of the negotiators. Secretary of State Baker has said repeatedly that peace, even the talks themselves, will clearly not be possible if the parties themselves do not have a will for peace. Yet, even this apparently essential ingredient may not be present, at least not in a positive sense. Instead, the apparent willingness to engage in the peace process has been the result of the exigencies of the situation, when adversaries decide not that they do not want to continue the battle, but, rather, that they cannot continue. In a war situation this is usually decided by virtue of a military defeat or a series of military and possibly political defeats. In the Arab-Israeli case, however, it is not a matter of a defeat—of a victor and a loser. One might argue that the Arab side has become the victor politically, possibly morally, even though Israel has repeatedly been the victor militarily. In fact, this is not a situation of clear defeat or victory even politically or morally. As in the case of a number of wars (in Afghanistan, Angola, Korea), it is not a matter of the parties concerned being determined to reach a peace agreement. The parties concerned are reluctant and ambivalent about the necessity of talking. This description would apply in particular to the Syrian-Israeli situation.

This is not to say that there is no incentive for reaching an accord. It is, however, an incentive that comes as much from outside as from inside. Outside pressures (from the United States) are intimately connected with economic as well as political costs and risks, which outweigh the perceived benefits of continued struggle. While Syria and Israel may both be making such a calculation, the one—perhaps only—party which has reached the conclusion that peace talks are more worthwhile than continued struggle is the Palestinian side. Its participation is, therefore, far less reluctant than that of the states involved, albeit complicated by the existence of segments of the Palestinian public that have not yet reached this conclusion. Such a situation is somewhat typical for a national liberation movement and the conclusion of a war of national liberation. In such situations, armed struggle is designed to give way at some point to political talks in order to achieve self-determination in some form. It has often been the case with regard to national liberation struggles that (1) the state involved remains unwilling to concede, (2) an outside power or powers intercede while, (3) the movement itself displays a willingness to compromise in favor, for example, of a solution by stages. This description would apply to the Palestinian-Israeli situation.

The difference in the nature of the incentives for peace, deriving from the difference in the nature of the conflicts between Israel and the Arab states on one hand and Israel and the Palestinians on the other, would, therefore, explain the logic of the two-track approach. Such a logic exists even though this approach was initially proposed by the Shamir government in Jerusalem probably in order to avoid facing a united Arab front and possibly even to prevent the commencement of talks altogether, on the assumption that the Arab states would not agree to direct bilateral talks. Such an assumption was based on the belief that the Arab states, namely Syria and those beyond the immediate adversaries (e.g., Saudi Arabia and the Gulf states), would not be willing to accord Israel the recognition implied by direct bilateral talks. Similar reasoning seemed to render the additional, multilateral talks on regional issues even more unlikely. And indeed Syria has refused to participate in the multilateral talks so long as Arab-Israeli peace has not been achieved.

It was to avoid this chicken-and-egg approach, otherwise known as linkage, that the two-track approach was adopted. Solution of one problem would not be dependent upon solution of all problems. Yet linkage does seem to be implied. Syria has claimed that it will not make a "separate peace." Specifically, it has claimed that while it would be willing to agree to an end of belligerency in exchange for Israeli withdrawal from the Golan, it would enter a peace agreement only after Israeli withdrawal from southern Lebanon and resolution of the Palestinian problem. Israel will not withdraw from southern Lebanon without resolution of the Palestinian issue and peace with Syria, while Israeli fears of Syria motivate much of the opposition to giving up territory on the West Bank as well as the Golan. Virtually all the issues, therefore, would appear to be connected, almost as clearly as the regional talks depend upon resolution of the bilateral issues that would open the way to Arab acceptance of Israel in the region.

Such linkage may be the reason the solution can be sought in stages. And the stages on each front can be linked; indeed they may be intrinsically linked. U.S. thinking would appear to be along these lines, beginning with an interim Israeli-Palestinian agreement presumably for some form of autonomy characterized as self-rule. An interim accord is even conceivable between Israel and Syria regarding the Golan. The pattern might be similar to the Interim Agreement between Israel and Egypt in 1975, which called for Israeli withdrawal from only part of the Sinai and put in place security arrangements, outside (U.S.) guarantees in the form of observers, and arms and force limitations (for the areas concerned) up to virtual demilitarization. Staged solutions might, thus, give content to the idea of "process," which the U.S. administration values so highly, while actually putting in place much of the machinery of a final settlement.

The major stumbling block with regard to a staged solution is the issue of open-endedness. It seems unlikely that the Arab states or the Palestinians will accept stages (Kissinger's old step-by-step approach, which was embraced by the then Soviet foreign minister in May 1991)[1] unless the principles of an eventual, final accord were clarified or conceded in advance. The actual content of interim agreements might be easier to determine regarding the Golan, inasmuch as purely security (as distinct from ideological) considerations would be the subject. The major stumbling block regarding the Golan, however, is Israeli rejection of the principle behind the Syrian demand that any interim arrangements on the Golan be viewed as the commencement of Israeli withdrawal from that territory. This would constitute Israeli agreement to territorial concessions, and unless it were linked to interim steps on the West Bank and Gaza, it would not even constitute "territory for peace" inasmuch as the Syrians are (thus far) willing to offer only an end of the state of belligerency in exchange for the evacuation of the Golan.

The problem of the nature of the final settlement might actually be easier to overcome with regard to the West Bank and Gaza. The Camp David accords allowed for final disposition of the territory and the crucial issue of sovereignty to be determined after a five-year period of autonomy (negotiations that were to begin after three years of autonomy). Even the Shamir Plan of 1989 allowed for negotiations to be undertaken after a certain period to determine the final status of these territories. While the Palestinians would prefer to have the principle of self-determination acknowledged even in an interim accord, the clear delineation of stages, with the assurance of negotiations on the final status, would probably prove to be acceptable.

This is not to say that an interim accord between Israel and the Palestinians can be reached easily. Three immediate stumbling blocks are likely to appear when the parties finally overcome procedural issues and get down to substantive matters. The first may be a problem that arose early in the autonomy talks initiated (between Israel and Egypt) after Camp David: the issue of the source of authority for the self-rule to be conducted in the interim period. Would the Israeli government, or the Israeli army, be the source of the authority granted the new self-rule organs, or would it be Jordan or some outside authority such as the UN?[2] And a related problem would be the disposition of the Israeli army, in the territories, during this period, as well as control over internal security. A second, almost immediate, problem would be the geographic boundaries of the self-rule, i.e., would they include East Jerusalem or the inhabitants of East Jerusalem, or merely permit the inhabitants of East Jerusalem to vote and participate in the self-rule organs of the West Bank while excluding the city from the jurisdiction of self-rule itself? A third, equally difficult, problem would be the disposition of state lands in the territories during this period (some 60 percent of the land), the possibility of Israel continuing its settlement policy on these lands, or the possibility of a freeze on Israeli settlement and/or the creation of an authority (possibly joint Israeli-Palestinian-Jordanian) to determine the disposition of these lands during the interim period.[3]

It is not a simple matter to determine just where Israel stands on all of these issues or, for that matter, the more essential principles of a final accord. The government of Israel under Likud Prime Minister Shamir is ideologically motivated and therefore cannot be expected to agree to any territorial concessions regarding the West Bank. Shamir has consistently reiterated his devotion to the idea of "the Land of Israel" and his unwillingness to concede even one inch of this territory. Gaza and the Golan Heights, however, are not part of this historical territorial concept and therefore might be considered negotiable by the ideologically motivated government.

The sentiments of the Israeli public and numerous political parties, however, might indicate just the opposite position. The disposition of the Golan Heights is not, they would agree, a matter of ideology; rather it is a matter of security. And for the majority of the Israeli population and body politic, security—not ideology—is the major concern. Understanding this, and out of its own primary interest in security, the Labor Party has made a political issue of the need to hold onto the Golan. This in turn will render it difficult for the Likud to concede the Golan, although it would not make it impossible. It is generally believed, and probably true, that any accord brought by the government will be accepted by the public provided it points in the direction of eventual peace (as with the various accords with Egypt from 1974 through Camp David over areas previously claimed to be absolutely essential to Israel's security). Nonetheless, public concern over Syria's capabilities and intentions is very high; security guarantees would have to be convincing and preeminent to gain the Labor support necessary for parliamentary approval.[4]

Perhaps surprisingly, the West Bank does not present quite the same problem. The Israeli public, unlike Shamir, is neither ideologically motivated nor emotionally, religiously, or nationalistically tied to the West Bank. This is not to say that a large portion of the public does not view this territory as important for Israel's security. The small size of Israel and the strategic depth offered by the West Bank in the case of a future ground war are important factors for the majority of Israelis. Nor can it be said that the Israeli public is willing to see an independent Palestinian state arise in the West Bank, for Israelis do fear that such a state would be no more than an arm of or stepping stone for stronger, hostile Arab states such as Syria.

Yet, the Israeli public does appear to want and to be ready for a settlement of the conflict, even with the understanding that such a settlement must involve territorial concessions to the Palestinians (with or without Jordan). The growing recognition that a compromise is necessary is apparently a result of a process that began during the intifada, which intensified following the Scud attacks on Israel during the Gulf War, and which may in fact be climaxing due to the deteriorating economic situation in the country. The average Israeli is tired of the continued threat to personal security of terrorism and daily violence accelerated by the intifada. Sitting inside sealed rooms and wearing gas masks under nightly Scud attacks rendered people acutely aware of Israel's vulnerability and the nature of future wars in the region. And the unemployment and housing shortage caused in large part by the massive influx of new immigrants, in the face of large-scale investment and building of settlements in the occupied territories, aroused anger over the distorted priorities of the "status quo." Even Israeli security was perceived to be in jeopardy when the government called for a reduction of the military's budget, because of economic hardship, even as the diversion of large sums of money and resources into the settlements was greatly increased.

The public debate began to raise the question of settlements versus immigration, particularly once the U.S. government tied these two issues together regarding Israel's request for loan guarantees. The problem was not as Shamir occasionally sought to present it: the need for territory, i.e., space, to absorb the new immigrants. Rather it was the need to give up territory in order to absorb the immigrants, for the argument began to be phrased in the following manner: In order to direct Israel's resources to the creation of jobs and housing for immigrants and veteran Israelis alike, as well as to receive the outside aid and investment necessary for jobs and housing, Israel needs an end to the settlement policy and even peace itself. As various political circles put it, Israel was faced with the choice between *klita* (absorption—of immigrants) or *shlita* (control—over the territories). And such a dichotomy became increasingly clear to the public at large.

Public opinion polls conducted by the independent polling company DAHAF indicated the shift taking place in popular sentiment. Asked to list according to priority the issues the Israeli government should tackle, the largest percentage of Israelis polled (twice as many as the percentage for any other priority) placed the peace process as the most important issue for the government to undertake. The creation of jobs was the next urgent issue listed; settlements was last (ninth) on the list; that is, the smallest percentage of Israelis polled considered this a priority issue. In response to the question of what to do about the settlements should the United States claim they were an obstacle to peace, some 67 percent favored a halt or freeze of the settlement policy. It should be noted that only adult, urban, Jewish Israelis were included in these polls; kibbutz members and Arabs, if polled, would clearly have raised even this percentage. Most significant, however, was the surprising finding that of the people polled who identified themselves as Likud voters, some 59 percent (possibly 59 percent of Likud voters) favored a freeze or halt of settlements if they were an obstacle to peace. Indeed, a poll conducted by the Likud itself found that a majority (just over 50 percent) of the members of the Likud Party central committee favored territorial concessions on the Golan and in the West Bank.[5]

This is not the way Israelis vote, however, and it is entirely possible that these opinions will not be reflected in the results of the June 1992 elections in Israel. The reasons for this are twofold. First, the determining factor in the votes of many if not most people in Israel over the past fifteen years has not been ideology or policies but rather the attitude toward the Labor Party, which was in power from the founding of the state up to 1977. The hostility to Labor is widespread and deep-seated among a large mass of Jewish voters, mainly of European background. Labor has not yet freed itself from the unpopularity and stigma attached to it for what is perceived (not necessarily inaccurately) as discrimination and elitism, during its thirty years of power, vis-à-vis the "Oriental Jews," that is, the hundreds of thousands brought from Middle Eastern and North African countries or descended from Jews living in those areas. Second, there is general acceptance, in some cases only unconsciously, of the Likud's election slogan: "Only the Likud Can." While the Likud never spelled out what was meant by this, there is a general sentiment that only a right-wing government can bring about a peace agreement, primarily because it is believed that the right wing will drive a harder bargain and therefore obtain the best conditions possible for Israel. This attitude itself stems from the deep distrust of Labor and is one of the reasons that Labor, seeking to dissipate this idea, emphasizes its great understanding of and concern for security issues.

There are a number of ways in which the Israeli voter might overcome hostility to Labor and reject the ideological positions of the Likud. One may be the change that has taken place in the leadership of the Labor Party, bringing in Yitzhak Rabin. Precisely because Rabin, a former chief of staff of the Israeli Defense Forces (IDF) as well as a former prime minister, is perceived as "hawkish" and security conscious (particularly as a result of his harsh response to the intifada when he was defense minister), he has been polled as the most popular political figure in Israel. His nomination has indeed altered the polls, the most recent of which indicate a four-seat lead by Labor over Likud in the run up to the June 23 elections.[6]

A second possibility, not necessarily independent of the first, might be a situation in which the Likud is perceived as actually blocking progress in the peace process. This could come about only if Arab willingness to conclude a peace agreement and live in peace with Israel were clearly indicated in concrete and convincing terms sufficient to allay the suspicions and fears of the public. Sadat's visit to Jerusalem in 1977 was sufficient to do this regarding Egypt; some Arab move in the peace talks would, presumably, be necessary to put domestic pressure on Shamir. Divisions within the Palestinian camp and, in particular, the use of armed struggle and terrorism on the part of the opponents of the peace talks render such a possibility most unlikely. Indeed, the increased violence by these opponents strengthen the Likud's position, apparently justifying what might otherwise be viewed as unreasonable "hawkishness" on the part of the Shamir negotiating team.

There is the possibility, however, that sufficient domestic pressure already exists. Shamir's agreement even to attend a peace conference and the government's determination to keep the talks going may be the result of Shamir's appreciation of the public sentiment demonstrated in the above-mentioned polls. The more "dovish" position assumed by David Levy over the past year or so may well be due to this shrewd politician's reading of the public, including the Likud grassroots and middle-level officials (such as the mayors of Herzlia and Ramat Gan, among others). Whether this would be sufficient to overcome Shamir's ideological attachment to the "Land of Israel" idea is far from certain. Combined, however, with a public perception that the achievement of a peace accord is a genuine possibility, domestic pressure may force Shamir to alter his position or take some other step. Yet, so long as the government is perceived as acting seriously and responsibly in the peace talks, and the Arabs are perceived as recalcitrant or disingenuous, public sentiment in favor of peace will strengthen rather than weaken Shamir's position and that of Likud. In this connection the Likud is not only entering the election campaign in Israel as the "peace party," but it is also able to point to Arab and Palestinian terrorism as "proof" of Arab double-dealing, that is, putting up a facade of negotiating while continuing to pursue the unchanged goal of destroying Israel. And such a portrayal will be used to justify what might otherwise appear to be unreasonable recalcitrance on the part of Shamir.

There is one other factor, however, that could make a difference—the deteriorating economic situation in Israel. Growing dissatisfaction with the government on economic grounds may be, as noted above, increasingly linked with an awareness of the high costs of holding onto the territories and the continued state of war. Economic hardship would become particularly acute in the case of U.S. and European pressures, such as those that might be expected if the government were not forthcoming in the peace talks. The more drastic effects of such pressures, however, might become apparent only gradually, that is, after the next elections. It therefore remains to be seen just what impact the economic factor will have on political developments over the short run. Even without this longer-term, international factor, the Labor Party election campaign will focus on the economic issue in the domestic context (unemployment, poverty, failure of immigrant absorption) as the failures of the Likud government.[7] The center-left bloc of parties (the newly formed Democratic Israel[8]) will then clearly draw the connection for the voter between these domestic failures and the absence of peace, the economic and political costs of holding on to the territories, high investment in the settlements, and so forth.

The Israeli elections will clearly have a great impact on the peace talks. In the short term, they will effectively prevent any kind of progress or significant breakthrough before the elections actually take place on June 23. While the Likud would benefit from a breakthrough, as the "peace party," it nonetheless cannot afford to make the necessary concessions (assuming that it were willing to do so) for two reasons: (1) part of its campaign will be to argue that Labor, in power, would "give away" Israel's vital interests by making concessions; (2) its appeal must be to the right-wing voter who seeks a clear alternative to Labor (and may be attracted to the radical right). The Likud's position, and belief, has been that there is no need for Israeli concessions, that peace can be achieved in exchange for peace if and when the Arabs "understand" that Israel cannot be moved or defeated. While this need not rule out minor, interim moves (for autonomy, for example), it is most unlikely that Shamir would permit such moves at a time when they might blur the image of his basic position. And, indeed, the course of the peace talks in their first half year has demonstrated this unwillingness to compromise even on what appear to be minor matters.

The greatest impact the elections will have on the peace talks, however, will be in the long run. If the Likud emerges victorious, it will be able more securely to withstand U.S. pressures (and the accompanying economic hardships), confident of domestic support. Its positions, therefore, will not only remain firm but will also probably harden, not only because of its perceived mandate but also because it will presumably be indebted to the extreme right wing for creating and preserving a parliamentary majority and coalition government. If Labor should emerge the victor, quite another track could and probably would be taken in the peace talks, leading to agreement with Jordan and the Palestinians at least on some form of autonomy, including a freeze on settlements. A very real possibility is the emergence of no victor but rather a national unity government of both major parties. Just what policies such a government might pursue would depend on a number of variables, from the strength of the opposition (left or right) to the critical question of who would be the head of such a government. One could postulate a number of possible policies and scenarios regarding the peace process in these circumstances, but a national unity government seems unlikely to rule for a full term. Given the change in the electoral laws in Israel, whereby the elections after June 1992 will provide for direct election of the prime minister, there will be strong pressures and incentives for at least one party (Labor) to go to the electorate as soon as possible.

One factor that will remain constant, whatever the results of Israel's coming elections, is the role of the United States. Whether of a political, economic, or merely potentially economic nature, U.S. pressure is likely to remain the necessary, if not sufficient, element for peace negotiations. In the process of negotiations, U.S. pressure may well serve, perhaps only indirectly or implicitly, as the rationale or justification for the acceptance of measures difficult for either the Israeli or the Arab side to concede ideologically. With or without this element, it will probably be an outside party—namely, the United States—that will have to continue to provide the procedural solutions to the problem of keeping the various sides at the negotiating table when crises arise in the talks. It may well be necessary for the United States to provide substantive solutions as well, acting implicitly as a mediator even in what are actually direct talks. This would not, however, be the first time Washington played such a role in Arab-Israeli negotiations. Fortunately, in the new circumstances in the world, the United States can now fulfill this function unimpeded by Moscow. Indeed, the Russians, inheritors of the Soviet role, can be expected to assist the Americans, although Moscow's ability and capability to influence any party today are highly questionable. The United States, on the other hand, does have both the capability and, for the time being at least, the will to act. As in the case of Kissinger and the Arab-Israeli agreements of 1974–1975, and of Carter and the Camp David accords, so too in the case of a peace agreement today U.S. determination (for whatever reason) to settle for nothing less than success may well be the critical element for achieving a peace accord.

NOTES

1. Bessmertnych to Verejnost (Bratislava), May 2, 1991 (FBIS-SOV, May 9, 1991, p. 8).

2. Despite the fact that Israel was created by a UN decision, the organization is neither trusted nor respected in Israel, not by the public at large or by the government. The most recent source of suspicion derives from the "Zionism is racism" resolution of 1975, but in fact the distrust goes back to the days of Ben-Gurion, pressures on Israel to withdraw following the Suez-Sinai War, repeated and consistent failures of UN peacekeeping forces to prevent border incursions and terrorism against Israel, the immediate acquiescence and desertion of the UN

force in Sinai and Gaza prior to the Six Day War, and so forth. The "new world order" notwithstanding, the UN continues to be perceived by the Israeli government as an organization dominated by "pro-Arab" forces.

3. This last possibility was proposed, and agreed upon, by the Israeli and Palestinian participants in the Moscow conference, with the understanding that each component of such a joint authority or committee would have the right of veto.

4. Labor's votes in the Knesset would be critical for a majority, as they were regarding Camp David, because the extreme right-wing parties would presumably withhold their support for any accord involving territorial concessions, even on the Golan.

5. These results were not published in the Hebrew press, according to rumors, because the Likud kept them out of the paper; they were, however, reported on Israeli radio in one newscast and in the *Jerusalem Post*, October 11, 1991. According to a poll run by the Women's Trade Union NA'AMAT, by means of volunteers who reached over 80,000 respondents, 74 percent of the public favored territorial compromise on the West Bank and Gaza, and only 31 percent favored compromise on the Golan (*Middle East Mirror*, November 11, 1991).

6. Yediot Aharanot, March 20, 1992. (In fact the results of the elections gave Labor a twelve-seat lead.)

7. Another electoral factor to be considered is the vote of the new immigrants, believed to account for seven or more mandates. Without going into explanations regarding the characteristics and potential inclinations of the tens of thousands of mainly Soviet immigrants, recent polls suggest that these mandates will be divided three to two in favor of the center and left-wing parties, a shift from earlier right-wing tendencies. This shift is attributable to the immigrants' anger over the Likud government's treatment of their problems (jobs and housing).

8. Composed of the Civil Rights Movement, Mapam, and the centrist Shinui, expected to receive between ten and twelve seats in the coming elections.

5

Israeli Foreign Policy
After the Gulf War

SHIBLEY TELHAMI

The Gulf War of 1991 and the decline of the Soviet Union left Israel in a superbly advantageous position: Much of the military machinery of Iraq, Israel's most powerful Arab adversary, was destroyed; the Arab world was left divided and confused; and the inheritors of the Soviet empire were no longer in a position to offer an alternative to the United States.

While these considerations combined to give the government of Prime Minister Yitzhak Shamir additional confidence in its policy toward the Palestinians and the Arab states, there were also some reasons for concern that blurred the political picture somewhat. Essentially, there were three areas that raised questions about Israel's strategic confidence. First, there was the immediate concern about the spillover effect of the precedent set during the Gulf War in forging international consensus on the implementation of United Nations resolutions, as Israel feared that pressure would mount to implement UN resolutions on the Israeli-occupied territories. The second area of concern pertained to how the United States will define its strategic interests in the region in the post–Cold War era; will the United States need Israel as a strategic ally now that there is no fear of Soviet threat in the Middle East? The third concern pertained to Israel's economic difficulties, especially given the challenging task of absorbing several hundred thousand Jewish immigrants from the former Soviet Union. Still, these reservations did not outweigh the objective reasoning that gave rise to confidence in the Israeli government.

The immediate optimism in the Shamir government following Iraq's defeat was, in the end, based on calculations similar to those that gave rise to pessimism in the Arab world. Both Arabs and Israelis understood that the decline of the Soviet Union left the United States in a more dominant position in the region. The question, however, pertained to how the United

States would define its new role. While some analysts speculated that the U.S. commitment to Israel would now diminish with the decline of the Soviet threat, most Arabs and Israelis agreed that, in the end, U.S. priorities in the Middle East are set according to the domestic political agenda in the United States. Many Arabs agreed with Saddam Hussein's assessment[1] as he put it to his Arab colleagues before he invaded Kuwait:

> Given the relative erosion of the role of the Soviet Union as the key champion of the Arabs in the context of the Arab-Zionist conflict and globally, and given that the influence of the Zionist lobby on U.S. policies is as powerful as ever, the Arabs must take into account that there is a real possibility that Israel might embark on new stupidities within the five-year span I have mentioned. This might take place as a result of direct or tacit U.S. encouragement.[2]

Similarly, Israelis held the general view that the decline of the Soviet threat will reduce the importance of the Middle East in U.S. priorities even further, thus increasing the role of domestic U.S. politics in shaping U.S. policy in the region; and those domestic political considerations were generally assumed to favor Israel.

It is for this reason that both the left and the right in Israel had low expectations about the Arab-Israeli peace process. As a consequence, the Israeli government expected that its request for $10 billion in loan guarantees from the United States would not run into serious opposition: Why would the president of the United States risk a domestic confrontation in an election year when there are no pressing international threats? Thus, as indicated by statements of governmental officials and editorials in Israeli newspapers,[3] the Israelis were truly surprised when President George Bush asked for and received a congressional postponement to consider the loan guarantee request.

When President Bush took his unexpected stand on the issue of loan guarantees, the Shamir government presumably figured that President Bush's unprecedented popularity following the war gave him considerable domestic leeway in dealing with Israel. Ignored in the Israeli strategic calculations were international and regional expectations of political movement on the Arab-Israeli front, partly resulting from political commitments the United States may have made during the Gulf War. Moreover, as the United States strove to define a new role in international organizations like the United Nations, its lonely position on the Arab-Israeli question stood as an obstacle. Indeed, in the midst of the Gulf crisis, while the U.S. struggled to maintain the international consensus on Iraq, its position on the Arab-Israeli conflict (during the UN Security Council consideration of the Jerusalem clashes in October 1990) threatened to undermine the strategy on Iraq.

President Bush's position on the loan guarantees made it difficult for the Shamir government not to attend the Madrid conference. One interpretation of the Israeli government's intentions, commonly advanced by the Israeli left, is that Mr. Shamir was essentially "buying time" while President Bush still showed interest in the Middle East and while his popularity remained high.[4] But, although this consideration may have affected Israeli tactics, the Likud-dominated government certainly had an agenda.

LIKUD'S AGENDA

The Likud government had four strategic interests: protect its claims to the West Bank; successfully absorb Soviet Jewish immigrants; protect the economic, military, and political relationship with the United States; and, if possible, conclude separate peace agreements with Arab states. In the short term, these objectives had the following practical policy implications: the continuation of Jewish settlements in the occupied territories; the avoidance of any process that places territorial compromise on the agenda; the protection of U.S. aid to Israel; and the advocacy of bilateral agreements with Arab states, especially Syria. While all these objectives were not harmonious, the policy of the Shamir government could be characterized as one designed to avoid making trade-offs among these objectives.

Thus, the Shamir government was not entirely against a peace process but against a process that would force trade-offs. Some of its coalition partners, however, assumed that any process would inevitably force Israel to make compromises and were therefore opposed to the idea, with some extremists even arguing that peace treaties with Arab states are not good for Israel. For example, Knesset member Elyakim Haetzni, of the Tehiya Party, argued that formal peace between Israel and the Arab states is not especially desirable and that "de facto" peace, as now exists, is preferable:

> Egypt proves this case: 50 normalization agreements were signed but none implemented. Egypt even asked the U.S. to admit Russian immigrants so they wouldn't go to Israel; that shows that Egypt doesn't want Jews here— just like Haj al-Husseini in the past. Egyptian students learn negative things about Israel and their newspapers incite against Israel. The Egyptian ambassador deals in subversion on the West Bank. Egypt wants to destroy Israel by peace; Syria wants to destroy Israel by force—Egypt's method is more effective.[5]

Still, as the Gulf War ended, the Shamir government, despite reservations by members of the coalition, was especially interested in inaugurating bilateral negotiations with Syria. In general, the peace treaty between Israel and Egypt, and the military setbacks of Iraq, left Syria as the

Arab state with the most promising military potential. The Israeli public, while pleased with the outcome of the Gulf War, felt as never before the threat that modern missiles pose to the heartland of the state. Syria, with its Scud capabilities, was the object of concern. At the same time, the Israelis understood Syria's strategic vulnerability. Having witnessed what happened to Iraq and having understood the implications of the decline of their Soviet patron, the Syrians would desperately seek to avoid a confrontation with the United States and Israel. If the United States were to use its newly acquired leverage with the Syrians, what choice would the Syrians have?

In general, the Shamir government sought to focus the attention of any Middle East negotiations on Israel's relations with other Arab states and to downplay the Palestinian issue to the extent possible. As Likud Knesset member Benjamin Begin put it, "The problem is with [the Arab states] rather than with [Palestinian] Arabs west of the Jordan River."[6] At the same time, the Israeli government pursued the most ambitious campaign of settlement building in the West Bank to establish "facts on the ground" that would diminish the possibility of Israeli withdrawal. While some analysts viewed this as a commitment emanating from political pressures on a weak Israeli government from the extreme right, most believed that Shamir's own ideological commitment to this issue is unshakable. Some believed that Shamir's commitment to the West Bank was more important than his commitment to absorption of Soviet Jews or to Israel's relations with the United States.[7] But Shamir's strategy, in any case, was to avoid having to choose.

The implication of Israel's objectives for the Palestinian question was that Israel sought to separate the Palestinian delegation from the Syrians and also sought to differentiate Palestinians from the West Bank and Gaza from diaspora Palestinians. Since the Israeli government has never acknowledged the Palestinians as a distinct people who have a right to a state of their own,[8] the negotiations on the Palestinian issue were intended to address the presence of non-Israeli citizens in territories that Israel intended to make its own. Benny Begin put it this way:

> Eventually, Israel should apply Jewish sovereignty [to the West Bank and Gaza]. This can be done by decree. The legislation is already in place. . . . Autonomy is only for inhabitants, not for territory. And of course it is permanent not transitional. So the people of Israel have nothing to fear from Likud or the peace process.[9]

Implicit in this Israeli stand was the assumption that time is on Israel's side: Given that the Arabs have no military option, building more settlements in the West Bank and Gaza can only make Israeli withdrawal impossible in the future and the Arabs more realistic about what they can hope to achieve. To be sure, the Israeli position on what to do with the

Palestinian population appeared in flux. Most Israeli parties, including Likud,[10] opposed the marginal position of the extreme right that called for the "transfer option," which envisioned the forcible removal of Palestinians to Jordan. Likud's position on the issue appeared to be in transition following the Gulf War. In the past, Likud had been vulnerable to the argument from the Zionist left that keeping the territories with a large Arab population would eventually undermine the Jewish character of Israel—something that all major Israeli parties took to be sacred. Likud never presented a coherent response to this argument, besides offering the vague idea of limited autonomy and complaining about all the doomsday prophets of Israeli politics. But behind Likud's ambiguous position was a clear policy with an optimistic outlook. As Amos Rubin, the economic adviser to Prime Minister Shamir, pointed out, there was a strong Israeli hope that Palestinians in the occupied territories would find life so uncomfortable that they would decide to leave on their own, in large numbers. He suggested that, in the past, the economic policy in the occupied territories was partly designed to increase this possibility.[11]

But Rubin also suggested that the Israeli government's perceptions changed after the Gulf War. Israel, he pointed out, concluded that large numbers of Palestinians are not likely to abandon the West Bank and Gaza. For one thing, few departed in the past, despite the difficult conditions in the occupied territories. In addition, the tragic fate of the Palestinians in Kuwait (one of the most privileged Palestinian communities before the Gulf War) was a reminder of the frightening uncertainties of the diaspora. The worsening conditions in Jordan were also a deterrent to Palestinian departure across the river. In short, the Palestinians had no place to go.

Making the prospect of continued Palestinian growth in the occupied territories less threatening to Likud was the new prospect of large numbers of Jewish immigrants from the former Soviet Union; this prospect would work in favor of maintaining the demographic distribution strongly in favor of Jews for the foreseeable future. Thus, from Likud's point of view, the arguments from the Israeli left about the "ticking demographic bomb" that threatens Israel if the territories are not given up lost its bite.

The above considerations led Shamir, who had personally opposed the Camp David accords in the government of former Prime Minister Menachem Begin, to advocate Palestinian autonomy as envisioned by the Camp David accords. As expressed by Benny Begin, the new government position saw Camp David as "the only available diplomatic formula for making progress toward peace. . . . As Camp David is revived, it is important to emphasize the interim elements. There will be no progress if final status issues are discussed now."[12]

The expectation that Palestinians are not likely to emigrate also changed the Israeli perspective on the immediate economic policy in the

West Bank and Gaza. Soon after the Gulf War, the Israeli military administration took steps "to stimulate the West Bank economy"[13] (reduction in tax rates, raising of thresholds, Israeli investment in infrastructure)—steps designed partly to keep Palestinians at home and out of Israel. Palestinians recognized some small changes in Israel's economic policy after the war, but some dismissed them as Israel's attempt "to co-opt industrialists and shop owners in order to split the Palestinian community," or saw them as nothing new because Israeli policies typically "shifted back and forth between stifling and promoting limited Palestinian development."[14]

One can debate whether these modest changes in Israeli economic policies in the occupied territories were strategic in nature or merely tactical, intended primarily to pacify the Palestinians in order to avoid U.S. pressure while pursuing a bilateral agreement with Syria. Either way, the Israeli government appeared to have a long-term plan for the territories. Consistent with the Camp David accords, the government viewed the proposed five-year Palestinian autonomy as merely transitional. But unlike the Palestinians who saw autonomy as a transition toward Palestinian statehood, Likud viewed autonomy as a transition toward full Israeli sovereignty over the territories.[15] As to the status of the Palestinians under future Israeli sovereignty, "Likud would offer the option of citizenship to Arabs, as in Jerusalem."[16] Advocating such a position may have become more tenable with the new demographic probabilities arising from massive Jewish immigration from the Soviet Union, but it is hardly likely that Likud would openly advocate this possibility in an election campaign. By the winter of 1992, Labor politicians were already accusing Likud of choosing "Greater Israel" over "Jewish Israel."[17]

THE LABOR PARTY POSITION

While generally pleased with the outcome of the Gulf War like other Israelis, Labor politicians appeared pessimistic about the immediate prospects of Arab-Israeli peace. To be sure, many Labor politicians saw the end of the war as a fabulous opportunity to sue for peace with the Arabs, given the favorable regional and global configurations immediately following the war. But most politicians on the Israeli left based their pessimism on the continued popularity of Likud and their belief that Likud did not intend to exploit the favorable strategic circumstances in order to address the Palestinian question.

Whereas advocates of territorial compromise in Israel saw Israel's vulnerability to Iraqi Scud attacks as proof that territory is no guarantee of security in an age of long-range missiles, the Israeli right equipped itself with counterarguments. To the Likud, the Scud attacks showed that Arabs consider Israel to be on sacred Arab land. "Why was Tel Aviv a legitimate target for Scuds? Why did Saddam make an issue of Israel, and why did this bring so much popular support?" retorted Benny Begin.[18] The net result was to harden Israeli positions, especially given the Palestinian attitudes during the war. The Israeli peace camp was left confused. Avraham Shukar of the International Center for Peace in Tel Aviv noted that the Gulf War "created disarray in the peace camp, largely because of the negative image of the Palestinians that it produced. The peace camp also suffers from the absence of a clear strategy."[19]

The confused domestic Israeli sentiment entailed that the prospects for meaningful peace negotiations with the Arabs rested, on the Israeli side, with the plans of Prime Minister Shamir. On this question, Labor politicians were nearly unanimous in their verdict: Shamir will do everything he can to avoid a meaningful peace process. A typical Labor outlook on the prospects for the U.S. initiatives to hold Arab-Israeli talks in the summer of 1991 was the view presented by General Ephraim Sneh, former military governor of the West Bank and Gaza:

> The best case scenario for the current Baker initiative is that it is a photo opportunity. In the end, even if the conference starts, either Shamir will walk out, or central issues will be relegated to committees which will never meet. Last March, when Likud was debating how to react to Baker, one faction within Likud suggested to go to the conference, but then to find an excuse to walk out. This is still a possibility in the current initiative. In the end, there is no formula to satisfy both Shamir and Baker, because if Baker is to succeed, he has to deliver at least something to the Palestinians, which does not sit well with Shamir.[20]

This pessimism about the prospects of Arab-Israeli negotiations while Likud remained in power, coupled with the perceived stalemate in Israeli domestic politics, inclined some Labor politicians who were fearful of the consequences of government policies to suggest privately what they could not do publicly: Only U.S. "pressure" can help Israel out of its detrimental stalemate. As for specifics, the suggestions varied from withholding political support for Israel in international organizations,[21] to a more modest proposal for U.S. pressure to make Israel give the West Bank the opportunity to use investments coming directly from Europe and the United States.[22] Most Labor politicians, however, were reluctant to make such "unpatriotic" recommendations publicly.[23]

Labor's own support for the Madrid negotiations was anything but enthusiastic. Labor determined that Shamir will use the negotiations to buy time, defuse U.S. pressure, and prove to the Israeli electorate that they do not have to choose between U.S. aid, territory, and peace with Arab states—they can have it all. They were thus concerned that dragged-out negotiations would actually help Likud consolidate power. Their strategy was to attack Likud's priorities: ideology over security, settlements over economic well-being, and greater Israel over Jewish Israel.

More specifically, since Shamir's strategy was to stress bilateral negotiations with Syria and to downplay negotiations over the West Bank and Gaza, Labor politicians charged that the Golan Heights are more valuable for security than the West Bank, and that Likud is willing to jeopardize security for the sake of an ideological commitment to the West Bank; this position on the Golan Heights hardened with the selection of Yitzhak Rabin, whose "toughness" on security issues is one apparent reason for his popularity, as the leader of the Labor Party. General Ephraim Sneh expressed the emerging view this way: "I am ready for far-reaching concessions on the Palestinian issue, but less ready on security questions with Syria. I'm not in a hurry to make peace with Syria."[24]

Labor's reluctance to engage Syria in substantive negotiations and Likud's reluctance to engage the Palestinians left the Israeli public confused and many in the Israeli left frustrated. Three of Labor's allies in the opposition to the government—the Ratz, Mapam, and Shinui parties—decided to forge an independent alliance with the intention of being more aggressive than Labor in advocating peace negotiations and territorial compromise. There was also hope that the creation of a strong coalition to the left of Labor would move the center of Israeli politics to the left, thus enabling Labor to pull some votes away from Likud.[25]

Ironically, once the Madrid negotiations began, Likud, for its own tactical and strategic reasons, shifted its approach and appeared to emphasize the possibility of Palestinian autonomy, not a bilateral agreement with Syria. Probably motivating the Israeli government was the desire to separate the Syrians and the Palestinians, who on the eve of the negotiations managed to forge cooperative relations. The Syrian negotiating posture appeared much tougher than some Israelis had hoped. By luring desperate Palestinians with the possibility of a separate deal, frustrated Syrians could go it alone. But whatever the reasons for the shift in the government's approach, it took the thunder away from Labor's attacks.

CERTAINTIES AND UNCERTAINTIES
IN ISRAELI POLITICS

Certain Israeli policies are predictable even without reference to the domestic politics of Israel, and certain domestic elements in Israel are predictable without much reference to international developments. Israel's security policy, the military strategy of the state, the emphasis on the relationship with the United States, and the preference for a divided Arab world are all elements that have had continuity in Israeli policy, regardless of the domestic configurations.[26] Similarly, there are divisions, ideological commitments, and party loyalties that are almost unaffected by international events—a fact that helps explain the political paralysis of the last decade, despite important global and regional political change. But it is a mistake to overlook the substantially increased fluidity in Israeli politics that took place after the Gulf War.

Even Arab perceptions of the fluidity in Israeli politics changed after the Gulf War. To be sure, most Arabs remained suspicious of Israeli intentions, regardless of who controlled the government of Israel. But the old Arab view of Israel as a monolithic actor with singular designs that are divorced from domestic politics gave way to new thinking; so did the long-held Arab views that proclaimed that differences among the various Israeli factions were merely tactical, intended to confuse the outside world and achieve Israel's singular objectives.

A striking example of the new interpretation of Israeli politics was advanced by Bassam Abu Sharif, a key adviser to Palestinian leader Yasser Arafat. While noting that "it is unfortunate that the Israeli public is in a mood of occupation-continuation," he characterized the Israeli polity as being divided in the following way: 30 percent "extremists," 20–25 percent "democrats," and the rest simply backers of the official Israeli position. "Theoretically, if there is a new Israeli government with a different tone, the public mood would change within one year."[27] What is striking about this Palestinian position is not that it is accurate, but that the Palestinians pinned hopes on Israeli domestic politics; Israel no longer appeared a monolithic actor with predetermined designs.

Some Israeli politicians placed even more hopes on "the fluidity" of Israeli politics after the Gulf War.[28] There were generally five issues that contributed to this.

First, increased Arab willingness to negotiate and the emergence of recognized Palestinian representatives outside the PLO hierarchy undermined Likud's long-standing argument that Israel has no one with whom to talk. The sight of Arab representatives sitting across the table from Israeli negotiators was bound to have an impact on Israeli perceptions.

Second, the substantial economic costs of absorbing Soviet Jews and the deteriorating economy in Israel made the government's ability to attract essential foreign aid a major issue. Although Israel requested U.S. guarantees for $10 billion in loans over five years, some Israeli analysts estimated the actual Israeli need to be $30–$40 billion.[29]

Third, the uncertainty about the way the new immigrants would vote created new possibilities. There was no shortage of theories about the likely behavior of Soviet Jews. Some suggested that new immigrants will support the existing government to prove their loyalties to their adopted state; others argued that, since these immigrants are rejecting socialism, they could not bring themselves to vote for leftist parties; still others focused on the humanism and tolerance of this highly educated group of immigrants, which were said to incline them to stay away from right-wing parties; finally, there was the view that these are not religious and ideological immigrants, but ones who are seeking better economic opportunities in the West, and they would not support the Israeli government if they believed that governmental policy jeopardized their economic welfare. These conflicting considerations led some Israelis to believe that the Soviet Jewish vote in the early elections of June 1992 would be almost equally divided.[30]

Fourth, increased political efforts to raise the participation levels of Israeli Arabs in national politics raised hopes that this segment of the Israeli public, which constitutes 16 percent of the population, will make a difference. Although Israeli Arabs have generally been disorganized, which has undermined their influence in Israeli politics, the vast majority voted for Labor and parties on the left; this is not likely to change in future elections. But Israeli Arab participation in national elections has been much lower than their participation levels in local elections, and lower than Jewish participation in national elections; whereas 80 percent of Jews voted in the elections of 1988, only 68 percent of Arabs voted. One reason for the smaller Arab participation has been that Israeli political parties have not offered them much. But another reason has been Arab uneasiness (especially among Islamic groups) about participating in the politics of a state that is at war with the Arab world. The new mood of increased acceptance of Israel among outside Palestinians and Arabs raised hopes that more Arabs will vote, with the possibility of adding two to three Knesset members on the left.

Fifth, the Israeli public, frustrated with the disproportional influence of small parties, became more open to major political reform that could break the stalemate in Israel. Indeed, in March 1992 the Israeli Knesset instituted the direct election of the prime minister—a move strongly supported by the Israeli left, with the hope that it will diminish the relevance of small religious parties and increase the Arab vote. This change, however, could not be implemented in the 1992 elections.

How the above issues will affect Israeli politics in the next several years will be debated for some time. But, whatever happened in Israeli domestic politics, there were major changes that had occurred in Israel's international environment that neither the Israeli government nor the public could ignore.

INTERNATIONAL CHALLENGES TO FUNDAMENTAL ISRAELI POSITIONS

Many of Israel's long-standing foreign policy assumptions have been seriously challenged in recent months—a challenge that is likely to compel fundamental reassessment of policies, if not deep soul-searching. One of the most important components of Israeli foreign policy had been to cultivate and protect Israeli relations with Washington at almost any cost.[31] Many in Israel believed that the participation of the Shamir government in the Arab-Israeli negotiations was largely a result of trying to avoid an open confrontation with the United States. The negotiations themselves "have not been with the Arabs but with the United States."[32]

Yet, the Bush administration's refusal to grant Israel the requested loan guarantees before Israel agreed to freeze its settlement activity in the occupied territories helped bring about the most tense moments in Israeli-U.S. relations since the confrontation over Suez in the 1950s. Leaked reports of serious Israeli violations of the military aid agreements with the United States by the unauthorized export of U.S. technology added to the tension in the relationship. These events generated extensive debates in Israel about the future of the long-lasting and highly coveted relationship with the United States. Can Israel count on substantial political, economic, and military support from the United States in the future? Is the current strain in the relationship a fundamental shift in U.S. policy? Or is it merely temporary, emanating from an unfriendly U.S. president? Or should the blame fall on the shoulders of an intransigent Israeli prime minister?

While Israelis disagreed about degrees of blame, most agreed that the U.S. economic recession has made foreign aid unpopular in the United States, and that the end of the Cold War has made Israel harder to sell as a useful strategic ally—even if some Israelis hoped that a perception of a rising "Islamic Fundamentalist threat" could revive Israel's strategic utility.[33] Still, it was clear that, had the Bush administration decided to do business as usual with Israel, neither Congress nor the American public would have been likely to object; this was one of those instances when the president of the United States had considerable leeway.

Viewed in this way, President Bush's own attitude on this issue mattered a great deal. From the point of view of the Israeli left, some of whom had been asking for U.S. pressure on the Shamir government, the blame was to be placed squarely on the shoulders of an unreasonable Israeli prime minister who did all he could to alienate the president of the United States. From the point of view of the Israeli right, Bush (and Baker) were perceived to be anti-Israeli leaders, who exploited the global strategic shifts to display their hostility toward Israel; the election of a more favorable U.S. president could return U.S.-Israeli relations to normal.

While Israel appeared to be considering strategic alternatives to the special relationship with the United States, Israel did not really have viable alternatives—the military flirtation with China notwithstanding. This conclusion was bound to create soul-searching in Israel about the very policies that undermined the special relationship with the United States. On the other hand, one should never underestimate leaders' tendencies to rationalize detrimental policies: it was much easier for Shamir to hope for President Bush's defeat in the 1992 elections than to reconsider a course that he began in his youth.

But soul-searching is unavoidable for Israelis for reasons other than the relationship with the United States. The assumption that Arab states (other than Egypt) would never accept Israel was seriously undermined by the Madrid process; the long-sought Zionist goal of opening the gates of *aliyah* to the second largest Jewish community in the world appeared within reach; the world community signaled full acceptance of Israel with the repeal of the United Nations resolution equating Zionism with racism and with Israel's establishment of diplomatic relations with China and the republics of the former Soviet Union; the misery of the Palestinians next door continued to haunt, even as states like South Africa moved toward reform; and, ironically, just as Israel emerged at the pinnacle of its military superiority, its economic vulnerability and the dependence of its Zionist dream on outside support became glaringly visible. Tough choices have to be made: the electoral defeat of the Likud Party in the June 1992 elections showed that Israelis could not afford to rationalize all these issues away.

NOTES

I wish to thank the American Academy for Arts and Sciences for funding my visit to Israel and several Arab states in July 1991. Many of the interviews noted in this chapter were conducted during that visit.

1. In extensive interviews with officials, academics, and journalists in Egypt, Syria, and Jordan (in May and June 1990), I found a near-consensus on this issue.

2. FBIS-NES-90-039, February 27, 1990.

3. For example, Labor Knesset member Mordechai Gur said that "in his policy, Bush is showing signs of anti-semitism and anti-Israel tendencies" (FBIS-NES-91-179, September 16, 1991). Commentator Yo'el Marcus wrote in the Israeli newspaper *Ha'aretz* that President Bush's behavior was "tantamount to a declaration of war on the part of a President with whom Israel will have to live for another term" (FBIS-NES-91-178, September 13, 1991). Rehav'am Ze'evi, a minister in the Israeli government, accused Bush "of wanting to lead Israel to a second Holocaust" (FBIS-NES-91-184, September 23, 1991).

4. Interviews with Benny Temkin, secretary-general of the Ratz Party; Tamar Gonzanski, member of the Knesset, Hadash Party (Jerusalem, July 16, 1991); and Elazar Granot, secretary-general of the Mapam Party (Tel Aviv, July 16, 1991).

5. Interview, July 16, 1991, the Knesset, Jerusalem.

6. Interview, July 15, 1991, Knesset building, Jerusalem.

7. For example, this was the position taken by Knesset member Haim Ramon, head of the Labor coalition in the Knesset, at the Washington Institute for Near East Policy, on March 16, 1992.

8. Despite the reference in the text of the Camp David accords, which Israel

signed, to "the Palestinian people," a letter appended to the accords from President Carter to Israeli Prime Minister Menachem Begin stated, "I hereby acknowledge that you have informed me as follows. . . . In each paragraph of the Agreed Framework Document the expression 'Palestinians' or 'Palestinian People' are [sic] being and will be construed and understood by you as 'Palestinian Arabs.'" (See William Quandt, *Camp David: Peacemaking and Politics* (Washington, D.C.: The Brookings Institution, 1986).

9. Interview, July 16, 1991, Jerusalem.

10. In the interview with Benny Begin, he stated that he "very strongly opposed transfer. This will never happen" (Jerusalem, July 16, 1991).

11. Interview, July 17, 1991, Truman Institute, Jerusalem.

12. Interview, July 16, 1991.

13. Interview with Amos Rubin, Jerusalem, July 17, 1991.

14. Interview with Gahssan al-Khatib, Jerusalem Media Communication Center, Jerusalem, July 18, 1991.

15. Interview with Benny Begin.

16. Ibid.

17. Labor member of the Knesset Haim Ramon, the Washington Institute for Near East Policy, March 16, 1992.

18. Interview, Jerusalem, July 16, 1991.

19. Interview, Tel Aviv, July 17, 1991.

20. Interview, Tel Aviv, July 17, 1991.

21. These suggestions were made by several members of the Knesset in interviews in June 1990. Benny Temkin of the Ratz Party suggested that "the only real influence on Israeli occupation policies will be U.S. pressure." He went on to suggest economic pressure as an instrument of policy (interview, Jerusalem, July 16, 1991).

22. Interview with Elazar Granot, secretary-general of the Mapam Party, Tel Aviv, July 16, 1991.

23. It is ironic that Israeli politicians expected U.S. politicians to take domestic political risks on issues that were not especially vital to U.S. interests, while Israeli politicians were not willing to take political risks on issues that they perceive to be most vital.

24. Interview, Tel Aviv, July 17, 1991.

25. Interview with Benny Temkin, secretary-general of the Ratz Party, Jerusalem, July 16, 1991.

26. For a discussion of the enduring patterns of Israeli foreign policy, see Chapter 5 of Shibley Telhami, *Power and Leadership in International Bargaining: The Path to the Camp David Accords* (New York: Columbia University Press, 1990).

27. Interview, Tunis, July 25, 1991.

28. Benny Temkin of the Ratz Party was especially hopeful about the fluidity in Israeli domestic politics (Jerusalem, July 16, 1991).

29. Interview with Elazar Granot, secretary-general of Mapam (Tel Aviv, July 16, 1991).

30. For example, this was the position of Labor Knesset member Haim Ramon on March 16, 1992 (Washington Institute for Near East Policy, Washington, D.C.).

31. For a discussion of this component of Israeli policy, see Telhami, *Power and Leadership*, pp. 111-123.

32. Haim Ramon, Washington Institute, March 16, 1992.

33. See, for example, the *New York Times*, March 22, 1992, p. 1.

6

The Negotiation Process in the Middle East

I. WILLIAM ZARTMAN

Negotiation theory tells us that negotiations can take place when the prenegotiations functions are in place and when the conditions defining a ripe moment occur or are created. These conditions are necessary but not sufficient, because, in addition, it takes human will and skill to turn them into diplomatic reality.

The six functions of prenegotiation are: cost and risks, requitement, agenda, participants, support, and bridges.[1] These functions are intimately related to negotiation itself but must be in place before actual bargaining over divisions and exchanges can take place. If they are not accomplished when the parties meet to negotiate, they must be done on the spot before the parties can proceed. The first three are items that must be established between the parties for fruitful communication to take place: assurances on the costs and risks of any proposed agreement, assurances that concessions will be reciprocated, and agreement on the aspects of the conflict that are susceptible to an agreement and on those items that will be left out (for the moment).

The second three refer to the parties themselves: agreement on a list of participants (and exclusions), construction of support for the process in the other party's camp, and the building of communications between the parties. If these elements are not present when formal negotiations begin, the substantive process slows down while they are being built. If it is impossible for the parties themselves to put these functions into place, a mediator may be required to serve as their repository for the time being. But when the mediator leaves, the triangle must be replaced by a bilateral relationship or the remaining process will collapse.

The confrontation in 1991–1992 between the U.S. mediator and Israel over the $10 billion loan guarantee for immigrant settlement housing has

63

been deeply unsettling for the process of building a triangular relationship. Israel overspends and overextends in every way, militarily and civilly. The Israeli experiment—the creation of a new developed country in the Middle East—is as dependent financially and militarily on the United States as Castro's Cuba has been on the Soviet Union. Like all other nations, Israel needs to learn to live within its means and within its boundaries. Its overspending is now aggravated by an irredentist policy that seeks to use immigrants from the former Soviet Union as pressure for civilian occupation of the West Bank, reinforcing the military occupation. U.S. loan guarantees underwrite this occupation and thereby undercut the U.S. government's own peace process initiative.

The two are inextricably linked. The peace process seeks to roll back the occupation, in exchange for security for all parties as the basis for a lasting peaceful relationship. The occupation seeks to roll back the peace process, providing neither multilateral security nor peace and offering nothing in exchange for the gains. The formula under which the Bush-Baker Mideast initiative has been prepared is "territory for security," a formula first expressed in UN Security Council Resolution 242 of 1967 and used as the basis for the Kissinger disengagements of 1974–1975 and the Camp David accords of 1978–1979. Settlements occupy the territory and make it unavailable as a trade-off for security and so invalidate the entire formula.

During the early stages of the negotiating process, none of the prenegotiation functions are in place between Israel and the Arab parties. A major purpose of the persistent efforts of Secretary James Baker, under the cover of attempts to get a purely procedural agreement to a meeting, is to build a trilateral relationship of confidence where a bilateral one does not exist. Many of these functions can only be built on the official level, although an open and constructive public discussion can encourage official thinking. However, the notions of costs and risk and of support can be constructed unofficially. Parties can show the other side that their fears of costs and risks of given agreements are groundless and that governments will not find public support for policies that justify those fears. They can show the other side and their own leaders that there is support for a peace process, even while supporting their own goals and interests in it. The peace movement in Israel has done much in this direction, and recent polls showing support for the current initiatives show an even broader base. Unfortunately, both the PLO and ordinary Palestinian support for Saddam Hussein in the Gulf War ran in the opposite direction. By expressing support for the peace process, the Palestinian National Council could also contribute to creating some confidence.

There is a role in the right direction for friends and relatives of the countries of the Middle East in the host countries of the current process, particularly in the United States—the Jewish, Arab, and Christian communities in the United States, whose concern is not the states of the region but the area that they too call the Holy Land. Dialogue and support among these three groups, which can then feed back into the Middle East parties, can be an important positive factor in preparing for negotiations. These communities, working together and working separately, have an important role in thinking creatively about solutions, rather than digging in doggedly behind the rightness of any one side locked in conflict. There are isolated instances of this kind of contribution by Muslim, Jewish, and Christian groups, but scarcely enough. U.S. citizens and U.S. interests are not party to the conflict, and therefore the appropriate U.S. position is support for the process rather than support for the sides.

Yet, as indicated, there are traps in the mediator's activities. Both sides expect to have the luxury of talking themselves into a deadlock and then being saved by the chairs, especially the United States, upon whom the blame for an imposed solution can then be heaped. The mediator's role is critical but misperceived by the parties, necessary but habit-forming and dangerous. There is little understanding of the fact that the United States has started out with no plan of its own, but simply seeks to keep the parties locked in their confrontation until they themselves work their own way out. Yet, it is tempting for the procedural conciliator, growing impatient with stalemate, to give in to the temptation to substantively mediate or even arbitrate. If it does so, it still must leave the parties with the impression that the stalemate-breaking ideas came from them.

THE NEGOTIATORS' CALCULUS

Negotiation and the creation of an international community is the process of exchange. It involves the redistribution of goods (outcomes) so that all parties exchange an unpleasant present for a better future. Parties need to feel better off with the promised new situation, or else there will be no incentive to sign and to hold an agreement. Mediators use carrots and sticks to bring out the perception of the present as unpleasant and the future as promising, for all. Both are required: the future must be seen as preferable to the present, and promises as well as pressures are needed. The stick needs to be associated with carrots, so that the promise as well as the pain can be brought out.

The carrot is the problem. The Middle East grows many sticks but fewer carrots, and the carrots that are there are homegrown for home consumption, not available for diplomatic trade. For example, whereas the European Coal and Steel Community, established after World War II as forerunner of the European Community, was based on an exchange of iron for coal and of acceptance for control of Germany, such tradable items are of short supply in the Middle East conflict. In international politics, Israel cannot be expected to give up what it holds just because it is "wrong" (any more than South Africa could have been expected to pull out of Namibia simply because the UN told it to). The challenge is not to punish Israel for its existence but to change its views of alternative futures.

The same challenge exists with regard to the Palestinians and the other Arab parties, each with its goals and interests in regard to the peace process. Painful, frustrating, or inadequate as the present situation may be, there is little incentive being offered to exchange it for an agreement that will merely make it permanent. If the only outcome attractive to and offered by Israel is a finalization of the present situation, tantamount to minority status in an enlarged Israel, there is not much inducement for Arab parties to participate in a search for appropriate exchanges. It is therefore only rational to hold out for maximum, idealistic, unattainable goals, since the alternative offered to the frustrating present is only its formalization. It is only when an improvement on the present situation is offered as a conceivable outcome that parties give up their unattainable ideals and settle for half a loaf. That glimmer of a possibility was what led the Arab parties into the Madrid conference, but the glimmer must be kept alive and made more concrete for the process to continue.

These elements come together in the definition of a ripe moment for negotiations. A ripe moment is composed of a mutually hurting stalemate, optimally marked by a recent or looming catastrophe (sticks), a way out (carrots), and valid spokespersons for all parties.[2] None of these conditions currently exist between Israel and the Arab parties. The Gulf War provided a recent catastrophe, but with different lessons for different parties, and, above all, the mutually hurting stalemate is totally absent. A key issue in the pre-Madrid maneuvering was over the valid spokesperson for the Palestinians. The thinking behind the Madrid process has been that the shape of the way out of the conflict should not be confronted directly but should be left up to the evolution of the process. These elements of ripeness must be supplied; even if the process argument is accepted, indications must be provided that the parties will improve their lot by moving toward a mutually satisfactory outcome in the peace process.

Inducements are in scarce supply. Like many other states, Israel has long taken its security into its own hands and therefore feels it has little need for assurances of security. Since the peace treaty with Egypt in 1979, the security threat to Israel has been greatly reduced, and diplomatic recognition by Arab neighbors does not add enough security to make a peace process compelling. Since the Gulf War, U.S. security guarantees have already been demonstrated, and further assurances can neither increase their value nor overcome the doubts of Israeli skeptics. Thus, the current formula of the peace process is not very attractive to Israel, and the most prominent carrot of the mediator does not improve its attractiveness either. Indeed, the whole formula of "territory for security," which fit the Sinai so well, is not sufficient for the West Bank and Gaza, where a displaced population and a new political entity also have to be addressed, along with land and peace between existing states. (That formula is appropriate for Israel's northern border, however.)

What other carrots are available to counterbalance the stick against settlements and make the peace process attractive to Israel as well as to the Arab parties? One could be U.S. support for permission for some Israeli settlers to remain in the West Bank, to balance the Palestinians living in Israel and tie the two territories together on both sides. A similar exchange was the basis of the Evian accords between the French and the Algerians in 1962.[3] The exchange could even be opened to more detailed negotiations, with the cutoff date or numbers for continued settlement linked to the amount of territory being given up.

A second is to use the multilateral nature of the conference to establish comprehensive territorial trade-offs. The fact that the West Bank is no longer considered to be a bargaining chip by the Israeli government makes negotiations very difficult. The Arab states have nothing to offer Israel to buy back the West Bank. They cannot make up the price in security, as seen, because Israel already has it in large measure and because Israeli possession of the West Bank provides more of it than does giving up the territory. Recognition too is nearly in hand and does not make up the price of the territory. The bargaining chip has become a valued possession, awaiting its legalization.

The only trade in kind involves the other territories. Bilaterally, the parties have nothing to trade off to produce a solution on individual boundaries. As in the case of the West Bank, neither Syria nor Lebanon alone has anything (or enough) to give to Israel to buy back its territories, and the "wrongness" of the Israeli position in international law is not enough to produce a withdrawal. Bilateral withdrawals are produced only by defeated parties, and Israel, though in the wrong, is far from defeated. Other than by unrelated side payments, by Israel or by a third party, the only way to buy a resolution on the eastern boundary is with a resolution on the northern boundaries. A more (or less) favorable disposition of the West Bank can be counterbalanced by a less (or more) favorable disposition of the Golan Heights and the Lebanese buffer zone. A more favorable arrangement for the Palestinians would be paid for by the Syrians and the Lebanese; a more favorable arrangement for the latter would have to be paid for by the Palestinians. While this fact can open creative thinking about the Mideast bargain, it also explains the little progress achieved for so long. Only this sort of trade-off can change the nature of the outcome from a zero-sum to a positive-sum encounter, and it is the one positive promise that is inherent in the bilateral nature of the multinational conference that the Arabs want and that Israel otherwise fears.

The only way out of this type of dilemma would be to rethink the terms of trade, opening the way to imaginative solutions regarding the juridical status of the West Bank. Currently three solutions are proposed: a sovereign Palestine, a Palestine federated with Jordan, or a Palestine autonomous within Israel. Sovereignty is clearly situated in each of these plans. In today's world, however, new and looser applications of sovereignty are being mooted, with regard to Europe and the former Soviet Union. A danger of loose sovereignty is its instability, creating more problems than it resolves. An imaginative notion of sovereignty must both meet problems and provide stability, or if not stability at least instability that leans in a more constructive and stable direction after the interim has passed.

A notion that bears further exploration is the idea of two sovereign states with joint customs and security stations around their combined external frontier. Thus, while Palestine and Israel would be sovereign over their own territories, they would share security and economic surveillance along the borders of the entire former mandate. This would give Israel (as well as Palestine) control and assurance over its security concerns on the West Bank, would create the beginnings of a cooperative regime over two fully independent territories, and would put into effect a common free trade area, if not a full economic union. Both sides could claim their maximum boundaries while occupying a defined territory—clearly a positive-sum situation.

A third set of inducements could be found in the institutionalization and multilateralization of mutual recognition and security guarantees through the establishment of an ongoing Conference on Security and Cooperation in the Middle East, built on the model of a similar conference in Europe (CSCE). Creation of such a mechanism could be used to help overcome Israeli objections to a continuing peace conference. It would also add a further dimension to both U.S. security guarantees and Middle Eastern security commitments by associating the United States and Israel in continuing regional discussions of security issues and problems. No longer would a peace treaty be simply a static commitment, as is the Egyptian-Israeli treaty, but rather a dynamic process. In addition to such longer-range notions of inducements and packages, there is the need to devise ways of overcoming initial logjams in the various bilateral talks so that momentum can begin. It would be helpful for the bilaterals to establish some ground rules lest hard-line positions and tactics be mistaken for general conference purposes and tones. An appropriate opening declaration would indicate an intention to negotiate continuously and in good faith, to seek peaceful resolution of conflicts and move toward peaceful relations, and to pursue working group meetings between public plenary sessions. Such a declaration would not prevent tactical manipulations, including delays and walkouts, but it would put them in a context of committed search for solutions.

Sources of early impasse in the Israeli-Jordanian/Palestinian bilaterals are the question of settlements and the danger of an open-ended autonomy, a step that may threaten to be permanent. If the Israeli government continues to refuse to halt settlements in exchange for any available Arab commitment, an alternative could be found in the revival of an idea mooted but not adopted in the post–Camp David discussions, that of an Israeli-Palestinian joint commission, which would pass on any use of public lands in the West Bank, whether for Arab or Israeli use. If this is not acceptable, an Israeli declaration that it would review its refusal to halt settlements if progress were made in the negotiations after an appropriate time—thirty, sixty, or ninety days—would be another alternative. Similarly, a reaffirmation of the Camp David timetable for the West Bank and Gaza— negotiations on permanent status within three years after elections, permanent status in five years—would help deal with the problem of open-endedness.

Sources of early impasse in the Israeli, Syrian, and Lebanese bilaterals include the questions of Israeli withdrawal and ultimate intentions. They can be dealt with by constituting two Israeli-Syrian subcommittees, one to deal with short-term questions of security and the other to handle long-term questions of peace, negotiating simultaneously. The first would negotiate a "Golan II" withdrawal, based on trade-offs involving geometric boundaries (meridians), settlements and military positions, and verbal transfer of sovereignty; the second would consider conditions of "Golan III" or a permanent status, as well as Syrian constitutional discriminations against Israel, freedom of migration, security in southern Lebanon, and other questions.

In the search for a comprehensive peace, the key will be a continuation of the Kissinger-Carter step-by-step process, but without leaving natural "breaking points" where a step could be frozen. Stages, like the phases of the Sinai withdrawal between 1974 and 1979, must be unstable and designed to "fall forward," leading to the next step and eventually to a stable comprehensive settlement. Thus, preliminary stages should not be tenable in the long run and should include an agenda for the negotiation of the next phase. One of any negotiator's biggest conundrums is when to handle "the Big Ones," the major intractable problems with no obvious solution. Resolved early, they could smooth the way for agreement on other issues; resolved late, they would allow for lesser agreements to build precedents, atmosphere, and stakes in completing the agreement. The latter logic is more persuasive: the biggest problems should be pushed down the agenda for later discussion. These include the status of the PLO, the permanent status of the West Bank and Gaza, and the question of Jerusalem.

Other carrots can be created. The debate on the peace process should include a search for these carrots rather than the vindictiveness that the loan guarantees issue has unleashed.

NOTES

1. Maureen Berman and I. William Zartman, *The Practical Negotiator* (New Haven: Yale University Press, 1982); Janice Stein, ed., *Getting to the Table* (Baltimore: The Johns Hopkins University Press, 1991).

2. I. William Zartman, "Formula and Ripeness in the Israeli Border Conflicts," in Zartman et al., *Mediation in Middle East Conflicts* (Syracuse University, 1986, Maxwell summer lecture series); I. William Zartman, *Ripe for Resolution* (Oxford: Oxford University Press, 1989).

3. I. William Zartman, "Les relations entre la France et l'Algérie," *Revue française de science politique* 14, no. 6 (December 1964), pp. 1087–1113.

7

A Helsinki-Type Process for the Middle East

JOHN MARKS

This chapter presents a discussion of how, conceptually and in specific terms, a process similar to that of the Helsinki Conference on Security and Cooperation in Europe (CSCE) might be established in the Middle East. The aim is to initiate a process that, over time, would lead to a whole range of cooperative efforts and to "normal" relations among nations and peoples in the region. This process would provide a basis for resolving or transcending seemingly intractable differences.

At the outset, it is important to note that CSCE is not seen as being directly transferable to the Middle East. Rather, CSCE should be viewed as a model—even a metaphor—for a long-term process that might provide a framework within which hostile nations could resolve seemingly intractable problems. To put it another way, CSCE demonstrates the possibility—but certainly not the inevitability—that permanent belligerence does not have to define the Middle East. Obviously, a process for regional cooperation and security would have to be adapted both culturally and politically to fit the Mideast's unique realities. The idea is not to blindly accept the European example but to identify and accept what works, to discard what does not, and to invent additional modes as required.

DIFFERENCES

In terms of building regional security, there are important differences between Europe and the Middle East that need to be understood but that would not seem to rule out a large degree of applicability of the CSCE example in the Middle East. These include, but are by no means limited to, the following:

• In Europe, even in the darkest days of the Cold War, governments maintained diplomatic relations and had a tradition of direct communication. Of the Arab states, only Egypt now has diplomatic relations with Israel; for the rest, what communication does exist is clandestine and often denied. In this context, simply getting the right parties to the table has so far proved to be an extremely difficult task.

• In Europe, while various parties at times challenged the legitimacy of certain states, no state's fundamental right to exist or its very boundaries were subject to serious question.

• Conflicts in Europe were essentially bipolar; in the Middle East they are multipolar and even more complex than those in postwar Europe.

• Europe had large numbers of academics, experts, and private organizations who grappled for years with the issues that eventually became the agenda for CSCE. Their private, unofficial efforts played a key role in keeping governments engaged in the CSCE process. In the Middle East, there is a much less developed network of academic and private organization expertise available to undergird or promote a similar process in the region.

• In Europe, CSCE was only one of several processes that addressed critical political and security issues. Other multilateral and bilateral channels played a critical part in settling East-West and intra-European questions. In the Middle East, there are few other processes, and none that can address regionwide issues. The full implications of this point are not entirely clear, but it does suggest that a full-blown Helsinki-type process in the Middle East might be overwhelmed in a way that CSCE was not.

BASKETS

The Helsinki Conference itself took place in 1975, when all the European nations except Albania, along with the United States and Canada, came together at the invitation of the Finnish government. The conference itself was preceded by several years of diplomatic negotiation and preparation. The conference launched an ongoing process that involved consideration of substantive issues in separate groupings or "baskets."

It would seem that the strength of CSCE was not in the conference per se, but in the unique flexibility of the multibasket approach, in which agreements were reached by consensus—and then only provisionally—until such time as the essential trade-offs became clear and acceptable to the participants. In the Middle East, wide participation would almost certainly require a flexible organizing approach that has tangible rewards, although not necessarily the same ones, for all parties. Participants in the process should probably be all the governments of the region; those national groups—specifically the Palestinians—with a stake in particular issues; and representatives from outside powers with important interests in the region and with a capacity to help achieve solutions to regional problems. The process would provide a framework, or umbrella, for parallel discussions on a wide variety of issues, or "baskets."

Baskets might include, but not be limited to, the following:

- *Security*: including arms control and confidence-building measures
- *Conflicts and Conflict Resolution*: including Arab-Israeli, Lebanese, Iran-Iraq, etc.
- *Civil Society*: including human rights, refugees, and people-to-people contacts
- *Regional Economic Cooperation*: including the environment and water

QUALITIES

The following reflects some of the qualities that were part of CSCE and that might well be included in any comparable process in the Middle East:

- *Something for everyone:* When CSCE began in 1975, each of the thirty-four participating countries had its own reasons for participating. The USSR wanted confirmation of post–World War II borders; Eastern Europe saw CSCE as a way to maintain contact with the West; the FRG saw it as validation of and support for *Ostpolitik*; Western European leaders, in general, wanted "wiggle room" in the struggle between the superpowers; the United States, while not enthusiastic, saw it as a forum to push human rights. Then, as the interests of the parties changed over the subsequent fifteen years, CSCE remained a broad enough framework to contain the participants' new perspectives and concerns. The point is that CSCE offered something different to each participant. It provided a framework for countries that did not want to talk about the same things to negotiate their most important concerns. In essence, each nation was able to emphasize what it chose, while participating in the overall process; each had its own incentives and found its own rewards.

In the Middle East, the aim would be to build a framework that, for each country, furnishes rewards and addresses issues of direct concern. For Israel, the carrot might be the prospect of holding talks with Arabs from all over the Middle East on a wide range of regional problems, not only on the question of borders. These might include arms control, refugee issues, or recognition by neighbors. For Palestinians, the process could present the chance to be involved, in some sort of "official" framework, in discussions with Israelis. Topics could include everything from national rights to refugees and "the right of return." For Syria, there would presumably be an interest in resetting borders. For Lebanon, the emphasis might be on ending the flow of arms to militias and otherwise limiting outside interference. In general, each country would be given an incentive to attend and to continue with the process. Those planning the process should be as responsive as possible to the wants and needs of all the parties.

• *Formlessness*: The relative formlessness of CSCE was perhaps its most innovative quality—and the one that distinguished it from other less successful initiatives. It operated by consensus, and no country had to agree to anything if it did not want to. Following this example, participants in the Middle East might start by seeking relatively "easy" agreements on confidence-building measures (CBMs). The idea would be to keep the framework broad enough to handle anything that might come up and to find some early agreements, which would have the effect of building confidence in the process. These could include noncontroversial CBMs along the lines of installing hotlines, ending a shared environmental threat, and cooperating to provide health care to sick children.

• *Flexible baskets*: CSCE had four baskets, within which virtually everything could be discussed. These were (1) security issues; (2) economic, technical, and environmental issues; (3) human rights and cultural cooperation; and (4) future follow-up sessions to determine if the agreements were being fulfilled. A Middle East process might establish general baskets, broad enough to hold any and all issues but with enough ambiguity so as not to lock anyone out. While the overall process should be as inclusive as possible, people from every nation would not necessarily participate in every basket, nor would the baskets necessarily meet at the same time. There could even be empty baskets whose existence might be needed to ensure participation of all necessary parties. Even if baskets remained empty, having them in place would leave open the possibility that a particular subject might be addressed in the future.

The multibasket approach would aim to produce the kinds of trade-offs between security, economic, and resource issues that might permit eventual settlement of key territorial issues. The multibasket approach would also provide a mechanism for embedding in the process difficult political issues without producing immediate deadlock. By working separately on discreet baskets, it is conceivable that confidence-building measures, for example, might emerge in a negotiation of water issues that would have a positive impact on consideration of security issues that were otherwise stalemated. In such a process, participants would be able to address individual issues within a framework in which they stipulate peace as the final outcome and then *provisionally* work through the obstacles to resolving the issue itself. Moreover, the provisional nature of the work might also provide incentives for reluctant participants to join the dialogue.

• *Flexibility in form and language*: The first CSCE accords were "politically binding international agreements," not treaties. This form was used to avoid treaties that, at the time, some feared would have given recognition to Soviet annexation of the Baltic republics or been subject to formal ratification processes. Using a different form made these CSCE accords more palatable, thereby making it easier to reach agreements. A Middle East process should also try to adapt new or innovative forms that could make it easier to find common ground.

• *Starting a political process*: CSCE provided a framework for East and West to resolve and lessen differences. The idea of a Middle East effort would be to start a political process that eventually produces comparable results. It should be noted, however, that CSCE was one of the smaller parts of a much larger process. These included bilateral U.S.-Soviet talks, multilateral negotiations (e.g., the Mutual and Balanced Force Reduction talks), and *Ostpolitik*. In the Middle East, a comparable process would have to stand much more on its own because of the relative scarcity of other channels for communication among adversaries. The initiative would not impede or preclude development of other mechanisms to deal with regional problems. Nor would it interfere with ongoing structures such as the Council on Cooperation in the Gulf, but it would provide a means for strengthening and broadening their work.

THE OFFICIAL PROCESS

In October 1991, Secretary of State James Baker, with Soviet cosponsorship, launched an official peace process. While the first priority of Secretary of State Baker, the prime architect of the process, is the Arab-Israeli conflict, his plans call for a broader, CSCE-type process. Baker has made clear that the process should be regional in scope, that all countries in the region and Palestinians should be represented, that the process should not only focus on Arab-Israeli territorial and security issues, but should also include a wide range of regional issues—from water to arms control.

One can only hope that the U.S.-Soviet-sponsored process will be successful in including as broad an agenda as Secretary Baker intends. However, the premise of this discussion is that, regardless of how that process works out, the Middle East needs and would greatly benefit from a regionwide, cooperative process—a process that makes use of innovative methodology and negotiating techniques to find fresh ways to reframe problems. This regional process should have a life of its own, broader in scope than—but certainly including—the Arab-Israeli talks. The problems of the Middle East are extraordinarily deep-seated and complex. Solutions and agreements will not come easily or quickly. A regional, cooperative process will almost certainly include numerous failures and take many years to produce substantial results. It should be remembered that the CSCE process had been in place in Europe for about fifteen years before it was credited with large-scale success.

CSCE contained an overarching vision of "Europe." The parties in the Middle East do not now share a similar unifying theme. The regional process should promote the vision of a Middle East where there is general recognition that peaceful, cooperative relations are worth achieving and are more attractive than the current deadlock.

PRIVATE INITIATIVE

CSCE itself was essentially an official, governmental process. But beginning a CSCE-type effort for the Middle East does not necessarily require the participation of governments. I am currently involved in organizing an unofficial, "shadow" process called the Initiative for Peace and Cooperation in the Middle East (IPCME). IPCME is based on the premise, demonstrated frequently in East-West relations, that "track two" or "citizen diplomacy" can pave the way for eventual government action.

The IPCME's aim is to plan, develop, and coordinate a series of private activities that encourage a comprehensive, multitrack approach to Middle East security and cooperation. If successful, the initiative will serve both to support the official peace process and to develop on the nongovernmental level a broad range of activities and relationships that promote regional security and cooperation.

While private efforts cannot substitute for governments in dealing with central issues of war, peace, and borders, such efforts can complement, undergird, and, perhaps at times, catalyze the official process. They can provide a forum and mechanism for governments to explore ideas on an unofficial level. A "shadow" negotiating process can relate immediately and directly to official negotiating activities, *if* there is an active process under way. For example, a security basket working group, informally constituted, could examine obstacles that need to be removed in the eyes of, say, Syria and Israel in order to work toward a peace treaty. The group might then identify a series of confidence-building measures that might move the process forward. It is anticipated that our informal process will operate alongside official negotiations and provide a forum for exploring innovative approaches that might be more difficult to develop in official channels.

In addition, there are likely to be areas for dialogue and negotiation that would also be important to a stable region but that would probably not be addressed in early official negotiations. The informal basket approach would be well suited for plowing new ground on such issues as environmental standards, human rights concerns, development of tourism, prevention of terrorism, and others. And if meaningful dialogue does not occur on the official level, the informal, unofficial track becomes even more important in preparing terrain that might ultimately facilitate the initiation of formal negotiations.

And, in the event of stalemate on the official level, private efforts can provide an alternative model that would help keep alive the peace process. At the same time, the "shadow" process probably will keep its distance from the official process and not become dependent on it.

PART II

THE POTENTIAL FOR ECONOMIC COOPERATION IN THE MIDDLE EAST

8

The Limited Scope for Economic Cooperation in the Contemporary Levant

PATRICK CLAWSON

This chapter examines the prospects for regional economic cooperation among the countries of the Levant—Egypt, Israel, the Palestinian areas, Jordan, Syria, and Lebanon—with assistance from the United States and the former USSR. The discussion does not treat the Gulf countries nor the "Northern Tier" (Turkey, Iran, Afghanistan). The major role for the former Soviet Union in Middle East economics is with these latter regions. The Gulf countries and the former Soviet Union together produce nearly half the world's oil, which forms the basis for extensive cooperation. Geography, common ethnic ties, and an excellent fit of industries provide the basis for extensive economic ties between the Northern Tier and the republics of the former Soviet Union. Within the Levant, the focus here is on cooperation between Israel and the Arab nations.

The main theme of this discussion is that the prospects for regional economic cooperation in the Levant are limited. Grandiose joint investment projects are less appropriate than small steps with immediate payoff, a number of which are proposed below.

ECONOMIC SETTING

Economic Situation of the Levant Countries

Economic theory would suggest that cooperation between Israel and its Arab neighbors should be quite mutually advantageous. The benefits from trade and investment flows are, according to well-established theory and empirical observation, greatest between countries that differ substantially. While the climates and natural resources base of the Levant countries are rather similar, the obvious difference is that Israel has a much richer endowment of physical and human capital, while the Arab states lack sufficient capital to make full use of their extensive labor forces. Under these circumstances, the goods that Israel can profitably produce differ considerably from those that its Arab neighbors can make competitively, and so there should be a good basis for trade, investment, and labor flows.

However, because the Israeli economy is so much larger than that of its Arab neighbors—Israel's GNP being 20 percent larger than that of Egypt, Jordan, Syria, Lebanon, and the Palestinian territories combined—the benefits of cooperation are likely to make less of an impact on Israel: each dollar gained will be a much larger share of GNP for the Palestinian territories or for Jordan than it would be for Israel. To make the same point another way, access to the Israeli market would increase 2,000 percent the potential market for a Jordanian producer, but access to the Jordanian market would provide an Israeli producer with only a 5 percent greater potential market.

Despite the many differences in their economic situations, all the countries in the Levant have been through difficult economic times in the last decade. Each nation is eager to return to the high-growth path it experienced in the past (pre-1973 for Israel and Lebanon, post-1973 but pre-mid-1980s for the other states). The common sense of economic problems provides a hopeful background for cooperation, insofar as cooperation can be shown to contribute to prosperity. A review of the situation of each country will demonstrate the reasons for the popular sense of economic malaise and the challenges facing each country, irrespective of the peace process.

Israel. After the 1973 war, Israel went through a troubling decade during which per capita real income fell and then stagnated at the lower level. Domestic output (GDP) per person rose, but so did the burden of servicing foreign debt, resulting in a decline of overall per capita income. In the mid- and late 1980s, Israel enjoyed increasing income and reasonably full employment, though at first the growth was "hothouse artificial," fed by an increasing foreign debt and a yawning budget deficit financed by rampant inflation. Since the economic reforms of 1985–1986, growth has been somewhat slower but more sustainable. As the prospects for the economy have stabilized, Israel's currency has strengthened vis-à-vis the U.S. dollar, which has increased the purchasing power of Israelis. Per capita income in 1990 in U.S. dollars was $10,000, compared to about $8,000 in both 1985 and 1970 (all data in 1990 dollars).[1]

The prospect of a million immigrants in the period 1990–1995 will require Israel to raise roughly $80 billion in capital if it is to sustain its living standards, according to the Bank of Israel.[2] Domestic savings and a continuing flow of aid at the same levels as in the 1980s will generate $55 billion of that capital, which will leave a $25 billion gap. About half that gap can be covered by a normal stream of borrowing and use of foreign exchange reserves. Israel plans to raise the residual $12 billion with loans guaranteed by industrial nations, primarily the United States. However, were such funds not available, Israel could raise most if not all this money on international capital markets, though the interest bill would be $200–$300 million a year higher and the loans would have to be of a short maturity (probably seven years instead of thirty in the U.S. loans). The immigrants will shift the population balance in the areas now under Israeli control from 62 percent Jewish in 1989 to 64 percent Jewish in 1995; because of the much higher Arab birth rates, the Jewish proportion would be 60 percent by 1999 failing continuing high immigration.

West Bank and Gaza. The West Bank and Gaza experienced rapid employment and income growth in the decade following the 1967 Six Day War. Both local output and income from work in Israel rose, with per capita income rising from $700 in 1968 to $1,500 in 1975 (in 1990 dollars).[3] In the next decade, however, between 1977 and 1987, income growth slowed precisely as the growth rate rose in Jordan, which serves as the economic reference point for many in the West Bank. Per capita income in 1987 was $2,000 in 1990 dollars ($2,300 in the West Bank; $1,600 in Gaza). Since the outbreak of the intifada, economic data are less reliable. It would appear that per capita income fell by 1990 to $1,500 in the West Bank and $950 in Gaza. The economic situation in the Palestinian areas deteriorated sharply in 1990 during the Gulf crisis, because Israeli employers dismissed up to 50,000 of their 110,000 Palestinian employees, either because of growing distrust between the two communities or because curfews made these employees unavailable for weeks on end.

Jordan. Despite structural rigidities, after 1973 Jordan enjoyed more than a decade of growth, driven largely by aid and remittances, which came to a screeching halt in the late 1980s. Jordan's per capita income (as measured in 1990 dollars) had doubled between 1975 and 1985, from $1,250 to $2,500. With the decline in aid and remittances, from an annual level of $2 billion in 1980–1986 to $1 billion in 1989, Jordan slid into deep crisis. In response, the government adopted a vigorous adjustment program, with IMF assistance. By the first half of 1990, the economy was on the mend, with real GNP rising 1.5 percent, led by a sharp increase in exports.

The Gulf crisis was a blow to Jordan; the economy went into decline in the second half of 1990, so that for the year as a whole, notwithstanding growth in the first half, real GNP fell 10 percent.[4] Per capita income, adjusted for inflation, fell below the level of 1965. However, the decline in GNP, which according to Jordanian government figures was roughly $400 million, was more than compensated for by European and Japanese aid, which increased by at least $600 million above the 1989 level. Furthermore, the Jordanian government wisely took vigorous steps to force the economy to adjust to the loss in income, rather than spending money it did not have to subsidize returnees who would eventually need to look for work anyway.

Egypt. Despite exceptionally favorable circumstances, Egypt experienced little growth in the 1970s and 1980s. Per capita income in 1990 dollars was $750 in 1970; it grew slowly and unsteadily to $825 in 1982, stagnated around that level until 1987, and has since fallen to around $700. Sadat's policy of opening to the West and limited economic liberalization gave some boost to the Egyptian economy, but these measures were implemented in only a halfhearted way and were overwhelmed by the negative effects of excessive government spending on subsidies and on an unproductive bureaucracy. What growth occurred was largely fueled by the remittances from Egyptians working in the oil-rich states, which went from $0.1 billion in 1970 to $4.0 billion in 1990—10 percent of GNP in the latter year.

Syria. Syria experienced rapid economic growth in the first decade of Asad's rule. Per capita income in 1990 dollars went from $1,200 in 1971 to $2,400 in 1981, fueled by large aid inflows that paid for essentially all military costs so that Syrians could devote their own resources to productive activity.[5] The war with Israel inside Lebanon in 1982 added to the military burden, while aid flows fell sharply and the Arab market for Syrian workers and products shrank with the drop in oil prices. Magnifying these external problems was the government's use of resources for inefficient, publicly owned enterprises. Per capita income declined slowly to $2,200 in 1985 and then fell dramatically to $1,200 in 1989 as Syria entered into a deep crisis. Since then, Syria's prospects have brightened remarkably, thanks to the roughly $3 billion in aid pledged in 1990 during the Gulf crisis and thanks to oil output that took off in 1990, reaching nearly 500,000 barrels per day by 1991 (worth $3.5 billion a year).

Lebanon. No reliable data are available concerning the Lebanese economy since the civil war began. In the mid-1960s, Lebanon was by far the richest Arab country other than Kuwait, with a per capita income 43 percent that of Israel.[6] At the same time, Lebanon's income would appear to have been less equitably shared than in other Arab countries, based on the fact that its "social indicators" (school attendance rates, life expectancy, etc.) were little better than countries with less than half its income, like Syria. Per capita income fell during the civil war to the point that Lebanese may make only half of what they did prewar and less than they earned twenty-five years ago.

Regional Economic Relations

The Arab nations of the Levant have remarkably few economic relations, other than the spread of smuggling from Syria to Lebanon resulting from the presence of 40,000 Syrian soldiers in Lebanon. Trade between Syria and Jordan, Syria and Egypt, and Jordan and Egypt was less than 1 percent of the total trade of each country in 1990. An economist could explain the many advantages of a common market instead of isolated small national markets;

of easy access by all to ports in other countries (Jordan to Syrian and Lebanese Mediterranean ports, Syria and Lebanon to Aqaba); of joint exploitation of water resources; or of a common electricity grid. To date, the political mistrust combined with misguided notions of national sovereignty have outweighed the economic advantages from regional cooperation.[7] With Egypt, the economic advantages of cooperation are less because of the physical separation between the Nile Valley and the western Fertile Crescent, but the political problems—especially Egyptian bureaucratic resistance to foreign economic ties—would make economic cooperation difficult in any case.

Israel has had little trade with the Arab world. Israeli trade with the West Bank and Gaza accounts for only 3 percent of all its imports and 16 percent of total Israeli exports; indeed, excluding goods imported into Israel and reexported to West Bank/Gaza, those areas absorb less than 10 percent of Israel's exports. By contrast, Israel dominates Palestinian trade flows, providing almost all imports into the West Bank and Gaza and purchasing 80 percent of their exports.[8] Israeli trade with the rest of the Arab world is essentially zero. The main reason is the Arab boycott, which began in 1948 on the establishment of the State of Israel. As a direct result of the boycott, Arab nations refuse to buy products that are produced in Israel or that have any discernible Israeli input. In addition to the direct boycott of Israeli products, there is an indirect boycott against firms of any nationality doing business with Israel or with identifiable Jewish owners, thereby inhibiting a wide range of commercial relationships, most importantly foreign investment in Israel. The indirect Arab boycott was weakened in 1991 as Kuwait essentially stopped enforcing the rules, and there are proposals to eliminate it entirely.

However, the history of Arab-Israeli economic relations suggests that caution is in order. Although Egypt removed formal discrimination against Israeli products in 1978, a whole array of administrative procedures has been used to limit trade with Israel. Israeli trade with Egypt remains insignificant because of barriers put up by hostile Egyptian bureaucrats and because of resistance to Israeli products by Egyptian consumers. Some Western and Israeli politicians had unrealistic hopes for Israeli-Egyptian cooperation after the peace treaty. These expectations were fed by economists who prepared detailed forecasts showing the profitability of prospective joint ventures in agriculture, textiles, and tourism, among other areas, while ignoring the barriers of mistrust that would prevent capitalists from investing their funds on the speculative prospects that peace would endure and consumers would buy products from their former enemy.

The greatest regional economic cooperation is between Israel and the Palestinian areas. Before the outbreak of the intifada, 110,000 West Bankers and Gazans worked in Israel, generating $720 million in income compared to $1,750 million produced in the territories (i.e., GNP was $2.47 billion; GDP was $1.75 billion). Furthermore, nearly all imports into the West Bank and Gaza and 80 percent of their exports came through Israel.[9] By contrast, trade with Jordan had shrunk to the point that in 1988 Jordan sold the territories a mere $10 million in products and bought $52 million in goods. The value of Israeli-Palestinian trade and the level of employment have declined because of the intifada and the Gulf crisis, but the West Bank and Gaza have been unable to generate alternative markets and employment. It is hard to say that the territories are less dependent on Israel than before; it is more accurate to say that ties to Israel remain as large a proportion as ever of a shrinking total Palestinian economy. The experience of 1988–1991 is a good example of two general principles: first, that economic cooperation profits most the weakest partners (and the Palestinians are the weakest in the region), and second, that political considerations overwhelm economics even when the economic situation is desperate.

WATER AND ENERGY

One of the most emotional issues in the region has been water supplies. Egyptian governments have devoted disproportionate attention to the slight danger that Sudan and Ethiopia might reduce the flow of water through the Nile. Any hint that Nile water would be sold to Israel has raised political storms in Egypt. Disputes over the Euphrates led to serious strains among Turkey, Iraq, and Syria in the late 1980s. Similarly, the issue of the Jordan headwaters and the Litani River has been political dynamite in Israel, Lebanon, and Syria. The Arab League's program for the Jordan River headwaters led to the great tensions in the region in 1965–1967, and some observers would see the issue as the direct precipitant of the 1967 crisis that led to the Six Day War.

The water situation today is most acute between the sea and the desert along the Jordan River. A sustainable annual water supply in the region encompassed by Israel, Jordan, and West Bank/Gaza cannot exceed 2.5 cubic kilometers.[10] Some of that water may be needed to flush out salts, so the exploitable amount may be no more than 2.0 cubic kilometers. The supply cannot be readily broken down between the different territories, because any such division requires judgment calls as to how much water from each common resource, such as the Jordan River, "belongs" to the various parties. The most important sources of water for the region are (1) the Jordan River system (much of which originates in Lebanon and Syria) and its main tributary, the Yarmuk (which gets most of its water from Syria), which together supply about 1.5 cubic kilometers; and (2) underground aquifers (most of which are in the West Bank), which provide around 0.7–0.8

cubic kilometers, mostly from the aquifer that carries water underground to the Mediterranean Sea.

At present, throughout the Jordan, West Bank, and Israel region, water demand exceeds supply by 20–50 percent. The problem is particularly acute during the summer and during dry years, such as 1991. For the region between the desert and the sea, annual water use is currently about three cubic kilometers, approximately two-thirds of which is used for agriculture and one-third for all other purposes. The 4.5 million Israelis and Israeli settlers use about two cubic kilometers while the 5 million people in the West Bank, Gaza, and Jordan use about one cubic kilometer.[11]

As a result of the imbalance between supply and demand, the area as a whole is drawing down the accumulated groundwater supplies and is not providing enough water to maintain the level of the Dead Sea. Excessive consumption is causing the remaining water to become more saline, as seawater seeps in to replace some of the withdrawn groundwater and too little water is available to flush the salts out of irrigated farmland. Because of the water shortage, rationing has been imposed in parts of Jordan and may be introduced in Israel and the occupied West Bank/Gaza as well. The problem of water shortage is likely to become particularly acute in the Gaza Strip by the mid-1990s. Not enough is known about the underground water supplies to be sure how long present consumption levels can be sustained before they run out.

The serious problems of water shortage have led to claims that population growth cannot be accommodated or, more specifically, that there will not be enough water to accommodate Soviet immigrants and returning Palestinians. The obvious conclusion would then be that a political settlement must involve steps to limit the inflow of Arabs and/or Jews. These claims are flat wrong: the water shortage does not mandate any particular settlement of the conflict. Water is by no means an insuperable barrier to the region's economic development and population growth. The water balance is primarily an issue of the price at which supply and demand equilibrate. At a higher price for water, the demand would decline, and recycling (e.g., of urban sewage) would become more attractive.

There is a vast potential for reducing agricultural water demand. At the current extremely subsidized prices for agricultural water, farmers can make a profit from growing cotton, which is basically solid water; its production in a water-short region is a waste of a valuable resource. Ending cotton production would, by itself, be almost enough to bring water demand down to the level of sustainable supply. Furthermore, by charging a reasonable rate for water, authorities could induce farmers to change to less water-intensive crops and to use more water-saving technology.[12] Extensive agriculture uses roughly ten times as much water as industry for each dollar of income created. The water supply is quite sufficient for 16 million people, which is all the population growth that could be expected for the next twenty years under the highest scenarios for Jewish and Palestinian immigration. The only issue is whether there is enough water to sustain the levels of water-intensive agriculture desired. Over the longer run, a variety of more ambitious water projects (such as desalination plants or diversion from large rivers in the region) could be considered if the costs could be kept low enough.

Immediate Cooperation

There is already a considerable degree of common water use planning in the region. With regard to the Yarmuk and Jordan rivers, both Israel and Jordan adhere in practice to the Johnston Plan proposed by a U.S. engineer, with U.S. government backing, in the 1950s, though there are some important ambiguities in the plan.[13] This sort of cooperation results in a better situation for each than would unimpeded unilateral action. It is not clear that the same can be said for the water resources of the West Bank and Gaza. The Israelis correctly point out that some centralized controls are necessary to prevent depletion of the aquifer at an even more rapid rate than at present (residents of those areas complain, however, that Israeli settlers are allocated more water per capita than the Arab West Bankers).

There is undoubtedly scope for more cooperation in water use planning. Agriculture in the Jordan Valley, whether in Israel, the West Bank, or Jordan, is constrained by the lack of water during the dry summer months. Agricultural output could be increased if the winter flow in the river were stored for use during the dry season. Jordan and Syria have agreed on the construction of a dam, called Unity (Wahda) Dam, at Maqarin on the Yarmuk River, where it forms the boundary between Syria and Jordan. Informal negotiations have been under way between Israel and Jordan about the prospective Unity Dam, so far without results. The Jordanians have been quite unrealistic regarding at least two points. First, they thought they could avoid an agreement with the Israelis on the distribution of the water. That would have been unwise under any circumstances, and was completely unrealistic given that the Jordanians need financing from international aid agencies, led by the World Bank, whose clearly announced and long-held policy is not to finance a dam if there are disputes over the rights to its water. This policy has nothing to do with Middle Eastern politics; indeed, it was adopted after disputes in South Asia. Though all that the Jordanians would have to conclude with Israel is a formal statement of nonobjection, they themselves seem offended that the United States has not secured a waiver of this requirement.

Second, the Jordanians seem to think that the dam is none of Israel's business. Yet, the harsh fact is that any accord will have to address some of Israel's concerns arising from ambiguities in the Johnston Plan. For one thing, it is not clear that all sides have the same understanding of the

Johnston Plan or that the plan's assumptions about water flow are still valid after thirty years of development in the Jordan Valley. In addition, incentives must be created for all partners to curtail the salinity of the water, which has become a serious problem. Similarly, procedures are needed to reward those who reduce their call on the water during the season of peak demand.

Failure to compromise will hurt both Israel and Jordan and redound to the benefit of Syria. Most of the Yarmuk water actually originates in Syria, which does not use it and which has agreed to forgo its rights to the water in return for the electricity to be generated from the Unity Dam. If that dam is not built soon, Syria may reverse itself and use the Yarmuk basin water to develop the southeast part of the country.

Postpeace Cooperation

Of the various ways to increase water availability during the summer in the Jordan River drainage, the most economical by far would be to divert the Yarmuk into the Sea of Galilee (Lake Kinneret) and then pump the water into the Jordanian and Israeli irrigation networks. Such a scheme would provide water at a cost of around $0.01 per cubic meter, an order of magnitude less than other proposals. In the wake of a peace agreement, such a scheme would be among the most profitable forms of cooperation.

Regional water cooperation on a grander scale has attracted much interest. Many studies have been done of large regional water projects, such as water piped into Gaza and surrounding Israeli territory from the Nile,[14] a "peace pipeline" from Turkey, and large-scale desalination plants. Before billions are poured into any of these projects, their economics must be carefully studied, and the forecasts of project costs need to be reviewed. It appears that the cost of the water from some, if not all, of the large projects would exceed their economic value. Furthermore, because consumers now pay a price well below the economic value of the water, such grand projects would require huge subsidies unless water rates were raised sharply. Consumers pay as little as $.05 per cubic meter for water, while the marginal product value of water in the region is no more than $.20 per cubic meter,[15] and costs for desalination are at least $.50. As a means of providing the water for population growth and industry, these projects appear to have much higher costs than such alternatives as recycling urban water or, above all, curtailing the use of highly subsidized water in agriculture. As regards agriculture, few if any crops could be grown at a profit using such high-cost water.

A number of major projects have been proposed to provide water, power, or both—the two being intimately linked, since dams can generate electricity as well as store water and since thermal power plants that boil water to generate steam can be used to desalinize seawater. By order of apparent economic profitability (the first being the most profitable) and ignoring the many political problems, some of the major projects are:

• A tunnel from Lebanon's Litani River into the Jordan River would generate electricity (in the 500-meter drop into the Sea of Galilee) that would pay for a fair part of the project, which could cost under $100 million. It could also provide at least 0.1 cubic kilometer per annum of extra water for use in Israel, Palestinian areas, and/or Jordan; the amount of available water depends on how much of the currently unused 0.5 cubic kilometer in the Litani will be needed for future south Lebanese development.[16]

• A pipeline to bring Egyptian gas across Israel could be constructed at a cost of at least $100 million. The gas could be used to generate electricity for Palestinian areas or for Israel, and the steam-run electric plant could be combined with a desalination facility.

• Nile water could be pumped into Gaza, which currently suffers from water shortages and has few if any alternatives at as low cost as water from the Nile.

• A "peace pipeline" from Turkey could bring water to Syria and Jordan or, less economically, to the Lebanon/Israel/Palestine corridor.

• A desalination plant for Gaza fired with Egyptian natural gas might well be the second-least-expensive method for providing Gaza with water (Nile water being the first).

• A Dead Sea hydroelectric project, with water from the Mediterranean or Red Sea, would take advantage of the considerable drop in elevation, but would require long tunnels and/or pumping stations.

Before constructing any massive project, it would be more appropriate to consider limited regional projects. In light of suspicions about the intentions of other states in the region, no country will be at ease depending upon its neighbors for its vital supplies. It would therefore be best to design these projects so that they serve as backup reserves and/or low-cost alternatives; simultaneously each country would maintain under its own control facilities that could provide the water and electricity it needed, in a pinch. A good example of such a project would be connection of electrical networks, potentially extending from Turkey through to Egypt. Such an interconnected network would increase reliability of the system (if one unit went down suddenly, the network could provide backup supplies), and it could reduce costs (for instance, by evening out seasonal peaks, which are in the summer in desert areas and in the winter in cold Turkish areas).

A Final Thought on Water

Technicians cannot resolve the basic disputes about the region's water supplies. Regional water planning must ultimately allocate water on political grounds. There is no scientific or economic basis for determining a just sharing of water resources. All that can be done by economic science is to identify a broad band within which solutions would benefit each side compared to beggar-your-neighbor competition. Economics cannot ascertain the "right" allocation within that broad band.

TRADE

Nearly all economists agree that incomes throughout the region would be maximized by free trade and free flow of labor and capital, i.e., "open economies." The remaining question is how much "open economies" would increase incomes as compared with autarchy, with some economists arguing that the benefits would be small unless current restrictive policies by the area's governments are changed. The West Bank and Gaza would be left particularly vulnerable in a free trade zone in which its neighbors were protectionist.

The fact that the "open economies" policy maximizes incomes by no means ensures that it will necessarily be chosen by the parties: income is not the only desideratum in life. It is quite possible that the peoples of the region would prefer an option providing lower incomes but that would be politically preferable, e.g., an economy more independent from neighbors whom one does not particularly like. In the jargon of economists, the "social welfare function" includes many elements, and economists are ill advised to collapse it to income alone.

Some Arab business people feel that the advantages of trade with Israel are exaggerated. The importance of the wider Arab market—e.g., the Gulf countries—could make Levant Arabs reluctant to endanger their position in that market by trading with Israel. Even without a formal boycott enforced by Arab governments, Arab consumers may resist Israeli products and may prefer to trade with firms that are not heavily involved in commerce with Israel. Some Jordanian business people I interviewed in 1990 feel strongly that their country's trade future lies to the east, not the west, and would therefore hesitate before taking advantage of opportunities for trade with Israel. However, it is not clear how strong Arab consumer resistance would be; price discounts might win out over ideology.

Immediate Cooperation

The greatest potential for trade cooperation steps in the short term is for the West Bank and Gaza. Both Israel and Jordan seem to recognize that the economic situation in the territories is explosive, and hopefully they can be persuaded that easier access to markets in Israel and Jordan is one of the most readily available steps to increase Palestinian employment. The Israeli authorities took some steps in 1991 to ease their protectionist restrictions on Palestinian products that could compete with Israeli-made products, but these steps remain largely ad hoc and therefore subject to reversal at any moment without notice.[17] There would be little negative effect on Israeli producers and substantial positive effects on Palestinian producers if Israel were to adopt a general policy of licensing any Palestinian producer unless that producer poses a specific security risk (e.g., a rifle manufacturer). Jordan continues to effectively ban most Palestinian products by the unrealistic requirement that Palestinian producers cannot use foreign (e.g., European) inputs imported into the territories via Israel. Palestinian access to the U.S. market—which would be more important politically than economically—is seriously hurt by the silly U.S. rule that Palestinian products are not eligible for the substantial tariff discounts given to both Israeli and Jordanian products, on the grounds that the occupied territories are not part of either Israel or Jordan.

The proposals to end the Arab boycott would have considerable symbolic value for Israel. Paradoxically, the step with the greatest economic benefit may be that with the lowest political cost, namely, the end of the indirect boycott on firms that do business with Israel, as opposed to the direct boycott of Israeli products. The indirect boycott reduces the willingness of some foreign firms, most notably Japanese, to operate in Israel. Easier Israeli access to Japanese electronics products (and to sales in Japan) could help a wide range of Israeli high-technology industries. As for the direct boycott on trade with Israel, it seems unlikely that Israelis could in the short term overcome the consumer resistance they would likely encounter in the Gulf market.

The best prospect in the Arab world for trade with Israel should be with Egypt, which does not participate in the boycott. The Egypt-Israel experience demonstrates that ending formal barriers has little effect so long as the government bureaucracies retain their protectionist instincts and their distaste for their former enemy. If Egypt and Israel wished to improve their economic relations, they could readily consult on steps that would expand trade in a balanced manner. Obvious profitable steps would be to permit the sale of Egyptian produce and food products in Israel and of Israeli light industrial goods in Egypt. Such mutually advantageous measures are unlikely, because the high-cost local producers in both countries would object vigorously. An alternative approach would be to encourage joint investments, most obviously in tourism and textiles. The United States (unilaterally or in conjunction with other industrial nations) could more or less guarantee increased Egyptian-Israeli cooperation by agreeing to waive the current tight restrictions on textile imports if the textiles were produced from a joint venture. Again, such a step is unlikely because of protectionist pressure from the high-cost producers who would lose.

Postpeace Cooperation

A customs union for Israel, Palestine, and Jordan would benefit Palestinians the most by far. Part of the reason is that the Palestinians have the smallest market (a $2 billion GNP versus $4 billion in Jordan and $50 billion in Israel) and therefore have the most to gain from access to a larger market.

Another part of the reason is that the Palestinians already pay customs duties on goods imported via Israel or Jordan without getting any of the $100–$200 million generated in tariff revenue each year; by comparison, total government expenditure in the territories was $290 million in 1987.[18] Another part of the reason is that unlike the West Bank and Gaza, Jordan and Israel have obvious alternative markets outside the potential customs union, namely, the Arab East and Europe, respectively. To reach these markets, the Palestinian producers would have to pass through Israel or Jordan, which could impede access or raise costs through administrative barriers. Finally, the Palestinian producers are already subject to the full force of competition from Jordanian and Israeli products, while firms in Israel and Jordan are by and large protected far more from Palestinian competition. In a customs union, the Palestinian producers could be vigorous competitors who would profit at the expense of their Israeli and Jordanian counterparts (though, at least for Israel, the effect on the overall economy would be miniscule, given that the Palestinian GNP is so small relative to the Israeli one).

Palestinians would also be the primary beneficiary of more advanced cooperation among Israel, Jordan, and the Palestinian areas—what has been called the "Benelux" model after the cooperation among Belgium, the Netherlands, and Luxembourg. The most extensive form of cooperation would be a free flow of labor and capital, integration of utilities (like electricity and telephones), common transport facilities (including full development of Gaza Port and joint use of Lod and Amman airports), and a monetary union. By making more extensive use of the facilities of the larger Israeli economy, Palestinians would save on investment funds that could be then used to create badly needed industrial and agricultural employment. Furthermore, free flow of labor would make use of Palestinians' most easily exportable product, namely, its excellent human capital. Jordanians would also benefit, e.g., from the savings in capital costs and from the lower cost of using Mediterranean ports instead of Aqaba to reach the European market. But Jordan has already established some of these facilities and Jordan has less potential for some types of cooperation with Israel (e.g., labor export), so the benefits of the Benelux option would be less for Jordan than for the Palestinians.

The Israeli-Palestinian-Jordanian common market provides great potential for profit because the economies are so different and, as economic theory and practice have demonstrated convincingly, the benefits of a common market are greatest when the partners are strong in divergent areas. Similarly, a common market involving Israel and Egypt could greatly benefit both countries, since Israeli capital and technology could be combined with Egyptian low-cost labor. However, it is hard to see either the Egyptian or Israeli bureaucracies giving up their protectionist ways enough to permit trade on a significant scale. Nor is it easy to see politicians on either side agreeing to a combination of Israeli overseers and Egyptian hewers of wood and carriers of water, which would offend the sensibilities of both Egyptian nationalists and Zionists (an ideology that glorifies Jewish labor).

A more likely common market would involve Syria and Lebanon. Integration of the Syrian and Lebanese economies could have considerable benefit if the result were the marriage of Lebanese entrepreneurship and access to international capital with Syrian stability; but it could be a disaster if it meant a marriage of Syrian bureaucracy with Lebanese infighting.

CAPITAL FLOWS

Capital flows into the Levant have to date meant first and foremost government-to-government grants, which have been the main form of "aid" in the region. There are two basic problems with increasing aid flows, the first economic and the second political. Aid has been poorly used in the past to subsidize inappropriate investment, failing state companies, and food subsidies, and it may have hurt development overall by creating a culture of dependency. When aid is used to subsidize consumption, the result can be that workers scorn the jobs that the economy can provide; witness the complaints about unemployment in Jordan despite the presence of some 150,000–200,000 foreign workers.

In addition to the economic problems of aid, there would be major political problems as well. The Levant countries already receive much more aid than most countries at the same income level, and the pressures on Western aid budgets are already great because of the transformations in Eastern Europe. Furthermore, disputes would likely arise over what the aid goes to finance, as signaled by the controversies surrounding the loan guarantees from the United States for housing in Israel, held up for months over the issue of Jewish settlements in West Bank/Gaza. Jordan will have problems persuading its traditional patrons in the Arab world to provide any funding, much less increased funding, following the Gulf crisis. Syria is unlikely to continue receiving the kinds of subsidized loans extended in the past by the former USSR because of the successor states' economic problems and declining interest in supporting Syrian intransigence vis-à-vis Israel.

Grant aid is not the only form of capital flows. The Levant should be attractive to private loans and investment. Two fundamental barriers stand in the way of turning the region's significant investment potential into a reality. The first is related to peace: business people hesitate to invest in a region of perceived instability. A lasting and general peace settlement would have much more effect on restoring business confidence than would a partial agreement that leaves some issues unaddressed and that is not supported by some states in the region. To the extent that the decision to open up the economies to regional cooperation reflects a political commitment to a lasting and broad peace, then the "open economies" solution would be more likely to attract private capital.

Besides the problem of war risk, the second factor influencing private capital flows is economic policy: How attractive will these economies be for new businesses, leery of the reputation for strangling red tape and for misguided social welfare policies that discourage job-creating investment? Even in the most peaceful of circumstances, the Levant would not be as attractive to investors as are Eastern Europe and the booming East Asian economies, unless intrusive regulatory policies change. With fewer bureaucratic restrictions on business, the Levant is well positioned to attract foreign investors who want low-cost labor and warm climates near the European market, a combination not offered by either East Asia or Eastern Europe. The most likely investors will be those looking for access to European markets; one likely group with much capital to invest abroad in the next decade will be firms from the newly industrialized nations of East Asia. The burst of interest in the peace process shown by South Korean firms and the South Korean government makes excellent business sense. But the simple reality is that both a better business climate and less perceived instability are necessary conditions for more investment; neither by itself is sufficient.

One proposal for increasing capital flows, forwarded by U.S. Secretary of State James A. Baker, is a multinational development bank for the Middle East, evidently modeled on the existing banks for Africa, Asia, the Americas, and Europe.[19] Implementing the proposal would entail many problems, not least of which would be securing U.S. approval in the absence of Israeli participation, or Arab approval in the presence of Israeli participation. A Middle East development bank would at first seem to be an excellent instrument for funding the infrastructure projects that the area badly needs, as well as for promoting regional cooperative investments that no one government would undertake by itself. Unfortunately, a Middle East development bank would be of dubious help to any of the actors in the Levant.

For example, it is difficult to imagine how such an institution could aid West Bank/Gaza absent an agreement on which state governs that area, for the same reasons that preclude World Bank involvement in West Bank/Gaza. Recipient governments have always insisted that development banks obtain government approval for their loans, and lenders have generally insisted on government guarantees. Even loans from development banks to the private sector still require the approval of the concerned governments.

The bank would be of little use to Egypt, Jordan, or Syria, which are already struggling under a heavy debt burden. These governments have been unable to make efficient use of the billions in aid they have received, which raises serious doubts about whether additional aid would add much to development.

Of the players, it is Israel that could make most effective use of capital at market rates—to put its immigrants to work. The country's new labor, combined with the capital financed by the bank's loans, would almost certainly generate ample resources to repay the lending. However, there are obvious political problems with a bank that benefits primarily one side of the Arab-Israeli conflict. In addition, aid funds worldwide are limited, and it is not clear why they should go to Israel, which has a per capita income at least twice the cutoff for World Bank loans. Furthermore, it could be argued that Israel should borrow from international capital markets. While it had a substantial debt problem in the mid-1980s, Israel has not borrowed for five years while its economy has grown, and so its foreign debt is quite low—$32 billion, equal to three-fourths of its GNP or two years' exports. (By comparison, the heavily indebted developing countries have foreign debts equal to more than five years' exports.) Finally, if Israel is going to borrow from foreign governments, it would certainly rather borrow from the United States or other friendly governments than turn to an international organization with strong Arab representation.

Immediate Cooperation

The greatest barriers to capital flows in the region impede investment and aid in the West Bank and Gaza. Facilitating foreign investment in the occupied territories would benefit Israel by reducing the tension from high unemployment and falling income. In 1991 the Israeli authorities took a variety of steps to permit more capital flows, but as with trade liberalization, the measures are ad hoc and not clearly formulated or applied.

The single largest regional project under active consideration at the moment is the Unity Dam. As described previously, the Unity Dam would bring benefits to Syria, Jordan, and Israel. Under present plans, Jordan would have to pay the full cost of construction of the project. It is almost certainly infeasible to ask Syria or Israel to contribute to the project cost. But it should be possible to form a consortium of industrial nations that would pay for the dam as a grant if the Jordanians would agree to relax their position in the bargaining for a water accord with Israel. After all, the U.S. Congress authorized loan financing for this project at least once (in 1978). The cost would be several hundred million for a project that would bind together more closely three countries that have often been on the brink of war.

Postpeace Cooperation

Advanced industrial nations might wish to fund through grants an economic development fund that would implement regionwide projects. The concept would be that no one country is prepared to pay for the whole project because the benefits it would receive would not be large enough. However, arriving at a formula for sharing the costs would require such complicated negotiations that the project might proceed with great delay, if ever. The interest of the industrial nations would be to create ever widening economic ties among the countries of the region, so priority would be given to projects that require continuing cooperation. Were grant funds to be available for joint projects but not for independent projects, the incentive of free funds might well be decisive for reaching agreement on, for instance, rules for access to a common port at Gaza.

A Final Note on Capital Flows

Measures to facilitate the flow of capital face a paradox. The motivation for greater capital flows is likely to be a desire to improve living standards and to foster regional cooperation. Higher income and more cooperation would be advanced best by breaking down protectionist and autarchic barriers. But more aid could have the unfortunate effect of sustaining these barriers. To understand this perverse effect, consider the effect that more aid has. Aid finances the construction of infrastructure, such as roads and ports, and it underwrites government budgets. The motivation for cooperation is precisely to reduce the strain on such infrastructure and on budgets. The aid therefore reduces the need to cooperate, because aid makes possible independent facilities that would be unnecessary in the event of cooperation. In other words, the more aid, the easier to hide behind autarchic barriers and to avoid regional cooperation. In particular, the more aid offered to a Palestinian entity, the more likely that such an entity could afford to build its own infrastructure and to subsidize the population, rather than cooperate with its neighbors to use infrastructure together and to create a common market that would create more jobs.

REGIONAL POLITICAL INSTITUTIONS

At this time, it is highly premature to consider regional political institutions that might include Israel and other non-Arab nations. For one thing, the Arab League is an active institution that provides a convenient forum for addressing many regional issues. Because the League fills much of the need for regional coordination, the issues that would be left for another organization would be only the issues between Arab and non-Arab states. Those issues are precisely the most thorny in the region. In other words, a "regional UN" would be saddled with the area's worst problems without having an opportunity to forge ties of trust and cooperation by treating less controversial issues.

While it may not be realistic to envisage any political measures at the moment, it is important to establish what would be the first steps when conditions improve. One symbolic step would be to permit Israel to join the Middle East region in international organizations, ranging from the International Monetary Fund to the U.N. regional economic commissions.[20] Another step would be cooperation on a whole variety of transport and communication issues, where tacit cooperation is already the rule, such as air traffic control, allocation of the electromagnetic spectrum, and telephone traffic between Israel and Arab lands. This could tie into a number of potentially profitable regional ventures, such as a fiber optic connection to Europe for Egypt.

As for the more distant future, it may be possible to establish a regional institution along the lines of the Organization of American States (OAS) or the Organization for African Unity (OAU). Such a "regional UN" would be most useful if it included all the non-Arab nations of the area, especially Turkey and Iran as well as Israel. The record of such regional organizations as forums for addressing regional tensions is weak; witness the inability of the OAU to respond to the various Libya-Chad wars or the ineffectiveness of the OAS at bringing peace to Central America.

POTENTIAL ROLES FOR
THE UNITED STATES AND FORMER USSR

The main contribution of both the United States and the former USSR to Middle East regional economic cooperation would be as guarantors of peace, which is vital to investment and trade. These two great powers, which have provided the weapons and much of the finance for the region's military machines, are the only outside actors whose guarantees of peace will impress investors. Neither local nor outside capitalists are going to risk much money on regional ventures unless these two great powers have made visible and lasting commitments to prevent another Arab-Israeli war. Together, the two can also promote regional institutions.

There is little role for direct economic cooperation that combines the United States, the former Soviet Union, and the Middle East nations. To the extent that the Middle East countries would want to join with the advanced industrial nations in some special institution to promote joint development, the key actors will be the Europeans, because they are the logical market and source of much investment. Furthermore, the most appropriate way to involve Israel and the Arab lands in international economic cooperation with the advanced nations is not through some new special institution but instead through existing worldwide international organizations, like the IMF, the World Bank, and GATT.

Separately, the United States and the former USSR each can have some role in promoting economic cooperation in the region. The Soviets can have an important role as a trading partner. It is possible to imagine an enhanced Soviet economic role in the Levant because of the good fit. Israel is acquiring the world's largest Russian-speaking population outside the former Soviet Union; the immigrants bring with them an intimate knowledge of the Soviet market and the potentials of Soviet factories. The Arab lands produce the kinds of simple consumer goods in demand in the former USSR, which in turn has excess capacity in many of the simple heavy industrial products needed in the Arab lands. The USSR imported $2.5 billion from the Levant in 1990, or 3.8 percent of its total imports.[21] Exports to the USSR were most important for Syria, as the Soviet Union took 44 percent of Syrian exports.[22] Most of this cooperation, whether with Israel or with Arab lands, will thrive only if left to natural market forces rather than being forced by political pressures (which would make businesses suspicious that the deals may not be profitable). The appropriate role for the successor states' governments is to reduce administrative barriers to be generally supportive, as they have been with proposed airline coproduction programs with Israel.

The United States can have an impact on the region's economy primarily through investment. Part of the reason is negative: the United States is not a natural trade partner for the region, which is so much closer to the large European market. Part of the reason is more positive: U.S. firms have experience with Israeli high-technology industries, which have prospered from the high education level in Israel and from the sophisticated defense industrial base. As with the Soviet case but even more so, U.S. involvement in regional economic cooperation should come from the private sector, with the government role confined to reducing barriers and to providing general support, e.g., guarantees against war risk through OPIC.[23] Indeed, given the U.S. economic situation (record fiscal deficits, increasing foreign debt) and the poor record of the grant aid programs, the best role for U.S. aid to the region would be to shift to support for private lending and investment, e.g., through loan guarantees such as those proposed for the Israeli immigrant absorption program. Loan guarantees have acquired a bad name in the U.S. because of the negative experiences with the savings and loan and banking industries, but these guarantees in the Middle East, which should be fully paid for by charges to the borrower, can be justified as a way to offset the risk of war.

* * *

This chapter has offered a glimpse at some of the practical problems to regional economic cooperation in the Levant as well as some suggestions for limited and immediate steps. The aim has been to provide realistic and practical suggestions, in the hope of countering fanciful optimism. Economics have not and will not be decisive in Arab-Israel relations, nor indeed in relations among Arab countries. No one should expect the peoples of the region to put prosperity ahead of what they see as national security interests. It is worth noting, however, that the greatest benefits of regional economic cooperation accrue to the Palestinians, and that they are also the most vulnerable in the event of a move toward isolating the occupied territories from the Israeli economy.

NOTES

1. Unless otherwise noted, data are from the governments of the countries concerned, usually drawn from the International Monetary Fund's *International Financial Statistics* and the World Bank's *World Tables 1991*.

2. Bank of Israel Research Department, *One Million Immigrants—An Absorption Program,* April 1991.

3. An important element in West Bank output is the olive crop, which is much larger in even calendar years than in odd years.

4. Michel Marto, deputy governor of the Central Bank, cited in the *Financial Times,* May 31, 1991. Earlier, Finance Minister Basil Jardanah had estimated the decline at 8.2 percent, in the General Budget Statement for 1991, as printed in Foreign Broadcast Information Service, December 6, 1990.

5. The effects of the military on Syria's economy are examined in Patrick Clawson, *Unaffordable Ambitions: Syria's Military Build-up and Economic Crisis* (Washington, D.C.: Washington Institute for Near East Policy, 1989).

6. All comparisons of 1965 from World Bank, *Social Indicators of Development 1988.*

7. During the Gulf crisis, there was an interesting counterexample, in which political factors led to economic ties that were unprofitable. For roughly six months during the height of the crisis, Jordan stopped buying Iraqi crude oil under pressure from the UN coalition. Political factors led Jordan to import Syrian oil, which was not the least-cost solution.

8. The last available trade data are from 1987, prior to the outbreak of the intifada.

9. Israeli data do not clearly distinguish what proportion of this trade was foreign goods in transit through Israel and what proportion was trade with Israel proper.

10. One cubic kilometer is 810,000 acre-feet. One cubic kilometer per annum is equivalent to 31.7 cubic meters per second.

11. Haim Ben-Shahar, Gideon Fishelson, and Meir Merhav, *Economic Cooperation and Middle East Peace* (London: Weidenfeld & Nicholson, 1989), Chapter 3; and Hisham Awartani, "Agricultural Development and Policies in the West Bank and Gaza," in George T. Abed, ed., *The Palestinian Economy* (London: Routledge Kegan Paul, 1988).

12. Israeli and Jordanian authorities generally prefer to control water use by administrative orders rather than through price mechanisms. In early 1991, Israel adopted a series of steps to curtail consumption by the most water-guzzling crops, e.g., production of irrigated cotton was all but banned. These measures were a response to the poor rainfall in 1990–1991, but they are so sensible that they may end up becoming permanent. Jordanian authorities have been pressured by the World Bank to rely more on price increases for irrigated water, but they have also used a variety of administrative measures to reduce water demand.

13. It is unclear whether the Johnston Plan allocates shares in the river's water or absolute amounts, and whether its sharing formula applies to the water flowing by each second or allows for more water to be drawn during periods of peak demand.

14. Water from the Nile is already brought to El Arish in the Sinai, sixty kilometers from the Gaza Strip.

15. Economic appendix to *The West Bank and Gaza: Israel's Options for Peace* (Tel Aviv: Jaffee Center for Strategic Studies, 1989), p. 220.

16. Ben-Shahar, Fishelson, and Merhav, *Economic Cooperation and Middle East Peace*, pp. 72–75, 104–107.

17. Furthermore, some of the liberalization is accomplished by quietly permitting violation of the rules, a procedure that can lead to such unfortunate incidents of miscommunication as the July 1991 destruction of a multimillion-dollar facility in Baqa Shargiya (*Financial Times*, August 13, 1991).

18. *Statistical Abstract of Israel 1989*, data including the civil administration and local authorities' consumption and investment expenditures. Estimates of revenue from tariffs differ; cf. United Nations Conference on Trade and Development (UNCTAD), *Palestinian External Trade Under Israeli Occupation* (New York: UNCTAD, 1989), p. 85, and UNCTAD, *The Palestinian Financial Sector Under Israeli Occupation* (New York: UNCTAD, 1989), p. 94.

19. The *Washington Post* and *New York Times*, February 7, 1991.

20. Israel is now typically assigned to the European region in such organizations.

21. According to the International Monetary Fund's *Direction of Trade Statistics Yearbook 1991*, in 1990 Soviet imports from Syria were $2.16 billion, from Egypt $4.5 billion, and from Israel $.02 billion, compared to total imports of $64.89 billion.

22. The USSR took $1.96 billion out of Syria's $4.43 billion in exports in 1990, according to the IMF. The figure for Syria's exports to the USSR does not match that for the USSR's imports from Syria for technical reasons—the latter includes shipping costs, the former does not—and because of discrepancies in timing and coverage, which afflict the data from any pair of countries. The comparable 1990 data for Egypt were $0.41 billion to the USSR and $4.92 billion total. Israel reported a mere $4.9 million in exports to the USSR; Jordan reported none.

23. OPIC, the Overseas Private Investment Corporation, is a U.S. government–sponsored firm that ensures private investment overseas against political risk.

9

Regional Economic Cooperation in the Middle East

———— GIDEON FISHELSON ————

This chapter argues that peace followed by regional economic cooperation is the best, and most probably the only, way for the Middle East to resume economic growth and make up for the losses it has suffered in progress and betterment over the last forty-five years as a result of the state of war. We envisage two driving forces working for growth: first, the private sector, both domestic and outside the region, which is capable of responding to market opportunities once local governments give it a steady green light; second, the governments themselves, acting through regional projects for the production of public goods or public inputs and services. Some of these points will be spelled out as we proceed.

The following factors are justifications for launching regional economic cooperation: (1) the comparative smallness of Middle Eastern countries in terms of population, purchasing power, and size of markets; (2) the lack of traditional natural resources and the fact that existing ones are already being shared, or that sharing them would be the most efficient and beneficial way to use them; (3) the complementarity of available inputs, including technology and marketing experience; (4) the unique importance of nontraditional resources in terms of religion, history, and culture; (5) the geographic location of Israel, in view of the global trend to form economic cooperation areas that are geographically a tight unit and that are modeled on the European Community (e.g., North America, the Andes, Southeast Asia); and (6) the trend to join existing economic blocs (e.g., attempts by non-European countries to join the EC or to obtain certain membership privileges), while Israel already has free trade agreements with both the United States and the EC.

The Arab-Israeli conflict did not originate in recognizable economic causes. However, its economic costs have been, and continue to be, tremendous. The conflict has distorted the social and economic structure of the belligerents, has caused economic stagnation, and has made the Middle East politically and economically dependent on outside powers and resources (see Tables 9.1 and 9.2 for external debt figures and data on military expenditure). Its origins notwithstanding, economic arguments have emerged over time to justify the continuation of the conflict, e.g., control over regional water resources. Furthermore, in each country there are sectors that benefit from the state of no peace.

I shall explain as we move along that an end to belligerency and the establishment of economic relations with Israel ought to be a desideratum of all Middle Eastern countries. Economic relations might make formal peace more stable, or might precede formal peace treaties and help the peace process along. Such relations in advance of formal peace might replace the "balance of terror" with a "balance of prosperity." They are bound eventually to create a vested interest in peace, which would in turn be one of its safeguards. Bilateral business relations are likely to lead to interdependence. If business follows the market forces, the interdependence so created will be well balanced and accrue to the good of all participants.

By definition, benefits from economic relations—of whatever form— have a shadow price, also known as alternative costs and costs of dissociation. Letting market forces direct the economic relations would ensure that such shadow prices would increase over time and would reach a similar order of magnitude for all the parties involved. (This is, most probably, what Robert Schumann had in mind when he proposed to set up the European Coal and Steel Community in 1950.)

Needless to say, the paramount task of economic cooperation in the Middle East would be to strengthen peace and to protect the region from noneconomic interference likely to send it back to a state of war and to economic backwardness. The type of cooperation discussed here is peacetime cooperation, which would take place after the attainment of peace agreements.

This chapter presents a general view of the role of economic cooperation in terms of the well-being of the Middle Eastern economies and then goes on to stress the role of the private sector and to discuss the tasks left to the public (i.e., the governmental) sector. The chapter is both a summary of studies initiated by the Armand Hammer Fund at Tel Aviv University[1] and a look at them from a somewhat different angle.

THREE SCENARIOS

Our claim is that regional economic cooperation, with Israel as an active partner, is a necessary prerequisite for a Middle Eastern economic takeoff. We conceive of the area as divided into three circles, and though

Table 9.1 Total External Public Debt and Debt Service, 1987

	Debt, 10^6		Debt Service 10^6	Debt Service Ratio, % of Exports
	Total	Banks		
Egypt	34,515	1,351	1,495	17.1
Iran	NA			
Iraq	NA			
Israel	16,767	4,549	2,451	17.8
Jordan	3,518	1,010	518	21.7
Kuwait	0			
Oman	2,474	1,955	612	NA
Qatar	0			
Saudi Arabia	0			
Sudan	7,876	1,673	48	6.8
Syria	3,648	32	365	16.5
Turkey	30,490	11,011	4,576	31.7
United Arab Emirates	0			

Source: U.S. Bureau of Census. *Statistical Abstract of the United States 1990*. Washington, D.C.: 1990. Abstracted from Table 1483.

Table 9.2 Military Expenditures, 1987

	Total Expenditures 10^6	Per Capita $	Total as Percent of GNP
Egypt	6,527	136	9.2
Iran*	17,210	439	6.6
Iraq*	23,960	1,815	22.5
Israel	5,536	2,206	29.2
Jordan	650	220	13.9
Kuwait	1,330	714	5.2
Oman	2,052	1,235	23.3
Qatar*	830	3,597	9.3
Saudi Arabia	10,490	710	12.8
Syria	3,364	302	11.9
Turkey	2,890	55	4.4

Source: U.S. Bureau of Census. *Statistical Abstract of the United States 1990*. Washington, D.C.: 1990. Abstracted from Table 1486.
Note: * 1980 at 1987 prices.

cooperation might proceed gradually from one to the other, we suggest that it starts with what we call the inner and the median circles, while the outer one should follow not much later. (This is almost precisely the pattern followed by the EC.) Table 9.3 describes the three circles as we perceive them, with their implied economic strength. The division is, however, not a cut-and-dried one. Should Syria, for instance, be counted as belonging to the inner or the median circle? Should Iran be in the outer circle, or thought of as unrelated to any of the three? The division into circles follows the criteria of being similar in size and of having common borders. The latter would be the trigger for border trade, agreements regarding tourism, and initial stages of joint ventures. One also finds substantial complementarity (even in agricultural products) among the members of each circle.

The inner circle, the heartland of the Middle East, consists of small countries all directly involved in the Arab-Israeli confrontation. Their total population is only 12 million (unless Syria's own 12 million are counted in), and their combined land area is 47,000 square miles. The only similar area elsewhere is that of the Benelux countries, which have been cooperating

Table 9.3 Basic Data for Middle East Countries, 1989

	Population (000)	Area (Square Miles)
I. The Inner Circle		
Israel	4,371	8,000
Jordan	2,956	35,000
Lebanon	3,301	4,000
Syria	12,011	71,498
West Bank/Gaza	1,450	220
Total	24,089	118,718
II. The Median Circle		
Egypt	52,805	386,660
Iraq	18,074	167,924
Saudi Arabia	16,109	829,996
Total	86,988	1,384,580
Total I + II	111,077	1,503,300
III. The Outer Circle		
Iran	53,867	636,293
Gulf states	6,100	125,000
Sudan	24,476	967,495
Turkey	55,356	301,381
Total	139,799	2,030,169
Total I + II + III	250,766	3,533,469

economically since the turn of the century. In the United States, Ohio and Pennsylvania have a similar population and area.

The exclusion of Egypt from the inner circle is open to question. We have relegated it to the median circle because (1) most of its area is in Africa, thus not having a close geographical affinity to the inner circle; (2) it is considerably larger, in population and area, than the inner-circle countries; and (3) it has unique social, economic, and demographic problems.

Egypt shares the median circle with Iraq, and we would argue for the inclusion of Saudi Arabia in that circle, too, because of its close economic ties with Egypt and because of Jordan's dependence on the Saudi economy. If not listed in the median circle, then Saudi Arabia obviously shares the outer one with the Gulf states, with Sudan and Turkey, and possibly with Iran. The addition of an outer circle is justified by already existing strong mutual dependencies, such as between Egypt and Sudan and between Turkey, Syria, and Iraq (with regard to water resources), or between the Gulf states and Egypt, the West Bank, and Sudan, for whom the former serve both as a market for their excess labor supply and as potential sources of capital for various regional projects. Turkey, moreover, may well become a major supplier of water for Israel, the West Bank, Gaza, and Jordan (see more below).

Taking all three circles together (and even if we omit Iran and Sudan), the region seems large in terms of population and size. An expansion of these two factors is traditionally considered to stimulate economic activity. But size alone should not be allowed to mislead us. Most of the land is desert and poor in conventional natural resources (oil and the Dead Sea minerals are a different matter). Hence, prevalent natural conditions are not promising and, together with the continuous state of war, have led to economic underdevelopment.

Except for the oil states and Israel (which imported capital in massive amounts), per capita GNP in the region does not exceed $3,000. The nonresidential physical capital per member of the labor force is only about one-twentieth that of Western Europe or the United States, and the human per capita capital is about one-third that of the industrialized countries. Add to those statistics a population growth rate of more than twice that of Western Europe and the United States, and the picture of a backward region is understandable.

This being so, the region's only chance to compete and to catch up—despite past mistakes—is through economic cooperation. Cooperation, and cooperation alone, will increase the productivity of extant resources and amenities: human capital, climate, location, and historical and cultural uniqueness.

Among the arguments used in economic analyses to account for the presence of economic stagnation in developing countries despite their possession of vast natural resources is that they export their resources as raw materials. They get the scarcity rent but not the value added they would receive by converting their resources into usable, technologically advanced goods and services. Instead, the value added (several times larger than the scarcity rent) goes to the developed countries. This is true, to a large extent, for the Dead Sea minerals, for oil and phosphates, and for the products a gentle climate makes possible (winter fruits, vegetables, and flowers and winter tourism). As noted above, the inner-circle countries are small—too small to carry out advanced processing; or else they do not possess all the resources needed to produce and extract the value added. Regional cooperation is one possibility for overcoming this constraint.

Elsewhere, the world has found that cooperation does indeed offer a solution. Europe led the way; others followed suit, though they were not always equally successful. But one can cite the North American agreement (covering the United States and Canada, and possibly to include Mexico later on), the Andes countries agreement, the Southeast Asia agreement, and the constant efforts of non-EC countries to join the EC or at least to benefit from some of its privileges. Israel is in the latter category. The underlying reason for all these efforts is that one of the most potent economic stimulants is the size of the market to which a national economy belongs and which it serves. This might lead to the suggestion that each of the Middle Eastern countries will attempt to join, or become associated with, an extraregional economic bloc. But even if a Middle Eastern country should succeed in doing so (an uncertain proposition), it is not likely to benefit to any large extent. Israel has trade agreements with both the EC and the United States and derives various advantages from them. But these are but a small fraction of the benefits likely to result from peace and regional Middle Eastern cooperation. As it is, the benefits from joining an external bloc are limited because of the ongoing state of war, because of the geographic discontinuity between Israel and its trading partners, and because it is the end-of-the-line country. Any other Middle Eastern country would have the same experience, unless peaceful regional cooperation preceded its joining an external bloc. Peace alone would also be highly beneficial, but adding cooperation would increase the benefits significantly.

Things being what they are, the Middle East has shared neither the growth nor the increasing import/export ties that have emerged among the developed countries. Except for the export of oil and the import of military equipment, the trade of most Middle Eastern countries has developed at a lower rate than trade among the industrialized countries. Israel, and more recently Turkey, are the exceptions. Competing in the international market is not easy, especially for newcomers. But cooperation with neighboring countries does help (note the Southeast Asia agreement). Entry into the major leagues might, however, come sooner and at lower cost. Figures 9.1 and

9.1A summarize our view of the role of peacemaking and cooperation. The graphs denote expected broad trends. The actual gradients differ for various countries, but the sense of the curves is identical for all. The differentials in slopes are largest for the confrontation states, but are positive for all.

Figure 9.1 is the optimistic view. Figure 9.1A might be defined as more realistic. In Figure 9.1A the growth rates in the first years preceding

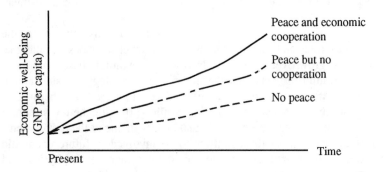

Figure 9.1 Economic development in the ME countries under three scenarios

Note: Peace, by itself, and perhaps even more so, peace and economic cooperation, are likely to require major adjustments in some countries, especially in the Arab countries, as armies are reduced and the structure of the economy changes. Thus, the curves might be somewhat U-shaped (see Figure 9.1A).

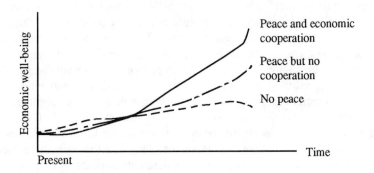

Figure 9.1A Modification of Figure 9.1

peace and cooperation are lower. The reason is the need to adjust to the new environment. Also, it is quite plausible that peace might negatively affect some sectors, e.g., those that produce for current military consumption. Cooperation that will eventually direct economic activities to follow comparative advantages might thus affect negatively the sectors and activities that suffer from disadvantages, with respect either to Israel or to other states in the region. In the longer run, however—more than three to four years—as the adjustment and transition period is completed, a steep growth will take over, the benefits from peace and cooperation will be realized, and those benefits will more than compensate for the adjustment costs.

The volume of economic relations is not a constant; rather, the potential for trade and economic transactions is an endogenous variable that is bound to grow over time. But already in their initial phases, the gains from trade, joint projects, and the transfer of technology are substantial. This is so because of the proximity of producers to markets and because of the possibilities of savings on cost, while providing better services. Proximity also makes for a better mutual understanding of the requirements and of the cultures of the countries to be involved in future economic relations. It also magnifies the resource complementarities of physical and human capital, technology, marketing connections, and local amenities and attractions. Such complementarities (e.g., food processing, textiles, clothing, footwear and other leather products, and a range of other consumer goods) are likely to augment the potential economies of scale and of larger local markets.

Cooperative ventures are not necessarily limited to adjacent countries, but a common border does help. Combining production factors from different countries with technological know-how and existing marketing facilities might improve the chances of a local economy to compete in international markets. Improved competitiveness would, in turn, cause the industries in question to expand. Relevant in this context are industries providing goods and services for which there is room in international markets; these could either be exported or used to compete with imports. It is here that the region has, or may develop, a comparative advantage. The decisions regarding which industries will be selected, who will enter joint ventures, details regarding factor usage, technologies to be applied, the markets to be addressed, and the method of profit sharing will all have to be left to the private sector and the operation of the market forces. However, the differences in economic systems, the many years of war, the present mutual distrust, and the doubts about the durability of peace all suggest that, at least in the early years, governments ought to give their backing to economic agreements.

The preceding passage might well sound too optimistic, especially to economists—as if we were saying that cooperation could work economic miracles. In reality, gains would materialize with different time lags and in varying volumes in different countries. Adjustment costs would also vary from country to country and might offset gains for quite some time. Some countries would eventually have to undergo a structural change, which might last several years and would not be cost-free either. Perfectly competitive intraregional trade implies specialization among Middle Eastern countries, and that too is a matter of time and adjustment costs. The real picture might well be that of a transitional period during which cooperation is circumscribed by internal policies and thus limited to certain products and industries.

The German-French model—analogous at first sight—is less so when more closely examined. The magnitude of the German and French economies, their internal strength, and their ability to adjust with minimal internal sectorial losses all distinguish those countries from those of the Middle East. Detailed studies are needed to determine (1) the capability of the Middle Eastern countries to adjust to a new intraregional structure and the cost—to each of them—of such adjustments, and (2) the ability of Middle Eastern countries to operate under a reduced government umbrella and to stand up to external competition. As long as this information is not available, one must accept as valid the hesitations of some countries to be thrown open to regional trade, and their insistence on a gradualist approach. In the short term, some may need a protective umbrella.

THE ROLE OF THE PRIVATE SECTOR

Middle Eastern economies are known to be under rather stringent government control. In many countries in the region, governments own and operate enterprises, or manage economic activities, that would probably work better if privately run. Principal reasons for this distortion are the continuous state of war, with the concomitant need to mobilize inputs; the implied risks that the private sector would shy away from; and the expected low rates of profit—another result of the region's fragility. Once the main reason for this is removed, privatization is likely to gather momentum. Obviously, private ownership should a priori be the pattern to emerge from an agreement to normalize economic relations on a regional basis. Governments will have to signal their approval, or at least refrain from discouraging it explicitly or implicitly (as was the Israeli-Egyptian case between 1980 and 1991).

The private sector, whether local or foreign (through multinationals), is looking for opportunities. In the past, the Middle East was not sufficiently attractive to outside capital and was not able to compete with other areas in terms of investors' expectations, partly because of the risks involved and

partly because of restrictive economic policies enforced by local governments (boycott laws or other constraints). Once these obstacles are removed,
the business climate is likely to change in a relatively short time (one to
two years) and the trend of investments from abroad within two to three
years. Once foreign investors realize that peace and cooperation are there to
stay, the region's growth potential and its unique geographical characteristics are bound to assert themselves. The local private sector will quickly
start to take advantage of the new economic freedom (say, within a year),
first through trade relations. Trade, after all, is the basic economic activity
between states. It also requires fewer and less intensive fixed inputs than
other activities. If it fails to work, and if this is understood before structural
changes occur, it can be terminated quickly, without great explicit loss to
the participants (though there would still be alternative costs). A case in
point—though various reservations must constantly be kept in mind—is the
development of the volume of trade between pairs of the original six EC
members between 1950 and 1970. I prefer, however, to use another model,
even though it is likely to elicit strong objections, including the charge of
irrelevancy: the volume of trade between Israel, the West Bank, and Gaza between 1970 and 1987. I am aware that the argument of there being no alternative will be put forward. I do not reject that argument, but I hold that the
recorded growth rate is high enough so that, even if institutional constraints
are taken into account, there remains a net rate capable of reflecting pure
"economic incentives." Having evoked counterarguments in any case, let me
take the matter a step further. To illustrate the benefits of economic cooperation, or at least of removing economic borders, we might look at the trends
of the GNP and of inflation in countries that have recently joined the EC
(Spain, Portugal, Greece). But let us remain in the Middle East. True, economic cooperation was forced on the territories. Did they gain from it, in
absolute terms? The answer is positive. Did they also gain in relative terms,
i.e., in comparison to what they might have gained had they been economically independent and had they traded with Israel under some form of economic cooperation? Emphatically no. The reason for the yes followed by the
no is that occupation implies constraints that prevent the attainment of the
unconstrained optimum. To be specific, if they were economically independent, the territories could have traded with the Arab world and established
any industry that seemed profitable. Until recently, these were controlled and
denied by the Israeli authorities.

The conclusion to be drawn from this section is that the Arab
governments have to do no more than declare that economic relations with
Israel are no different from those with any other country, and then stand by
their declaration. To prove their good faith, they would have to remove all
discriminatory barriers—in particular the anti-Israeli boycott—that now
stand in the way of normal economic relations with Israel. If they are

genuinely ready to act for peace, they should go a step further: all Middle Eastern countries should grant each other most favored nation (MFN) status. This was done by Egypt and Israel in May 1980 but was, unfortunately, not put into practice.

The May 1980 agreement should, in fact, become the common model for all such accords throughout the region. It terminates all boycotts, provides for the mutual recognition of official documents, holds the sides to compliance with standard sanitary rules, and allows for free participation in trade fairs and exhibitions. In addition, the Egyptian-Israeli transportation agreement of April 1982 should also be universally adopted. It allows goods to be shipped across the border in vehicles registered in either of the two adjacent countries (rather than in the country of destination alone).

Once such provisions are being put into practice, and are being reinforced by credit facilities and a foreign exchange clearing mechanism, the private sector, by now convinced that the way is open to genuine peace and cooperation, will come forward and step up its activities. This will result in increased volume and scope of such goods and services as are traditionally provided by the private sector in the West.

For those who prefer specific examples, let me list a few projects (other than trade, which is obvious) in which private entrepreneurs could cooperate:

- a natural gas pipeline from Egypt to Israel[2]
- an oil pipeline from the Persian Gulf to Gaza (see discussion that follows)
- fertilizer plants[3]
- joint ventures in textiles and clothing[4]
- tourist packages covering the entire Middle East, including transportation, accommodation, and guides[5]
- the production and marketing of winter fruits, vegetables, and flowers
- cooperation in providing transport services by land, air, and sea
- cooperation in providing high-quality health services

Let me expand a little on the Gulf-Gaza oil pipeline. About 180 million tons of Middle Eastern oil go to Western Europe each year, amounting to 30 percent of that area's annual consumption. About 80 million tons go to the United States, constituting some 5 percent of that country's annual consumption. It is, hence, entirely reasonable to suggest that, out of the total, 60 to 70 million tons might be shipped from Gaza and another 10 to 15 million via Israel.

Currently, world oil exports move mainly by sea. The supertanker (containing up to 300,000 tons) has made shipping competitive with pipelines. (One should, however, recall the environmental catastrophes in which supertankers have been involved, such as that caused—through human error—by the *Valdez*.) Some two-thirds of Middle Eastern oil moves by sea all the way, including all exports to the United States, Latin America, Africa, Southeast Asia, Japan, and Australia. Exports to Western Europe go partly by pipeline and then by tanker, or else move by sea all the way.

The carrying capacity of existing pipelines in the Middle East varies considerably, depending on the diameter of the pipe and the capacity of the pumping stations located along it. The Tapline, with a diameter of thirty inches, a length of some 2,000 kilometers, and a pumping capacity of about 100,000 horsepower, was designed to carry 25 million tons a year (0.5 mmb/d). The Yanbu' line has a capacity of 75 million tons a year (1.8 mmb/d), and the Eilat-Ashqelon line 6 million (1.0 mmb/d). The existing lines can therefore handle no more than a fraction of the exports to Western Europe, and so new ones have been proposed.

First to be mentioned is the proposed Iraqi line to Aqaba, designed as an extension of, or a substitute for, the IPC (Iraqi Petroleum Corporation) lines to Tripoli and Banias. The idea emerged against the background of the Iraq-Iran war, when Aqaba was Iraq's main port of entry for military imports. Furthermore, given Syria's hostility to Iraq, the line to Tartus was liable to be cut off at any moment. In peacetime, however, the Aqaba line is not economically justifiable. An IPC extension to Haifa would make a great deal more economic sense. But this is not the point at issue. The objection to the Aqaba line stems from the environmental dangers it poses to the Gulf of Aqaba and Eilat. In justification, the Jordanians might point to the Israeli Eilat-Ashqelon line, but that argument is not acceptable. The Eilat-Ashqelon line (previously carrying Persian oil, now oil from Egypt) is a major environmental risk itself and should not have been built there in the first place. The delicate ecological balance of the Gulf and the uniqueness of its marine life should not be exposed to additional risks. Its northern end should not be used for loading or unloading oil, and oil imports to Israel via Eilat should be stopped. The Gulf's northern hinterland might, however, be used for an on-land oil-linking terminal (the danger of spills from an oil transfer system is much smaller). Such a land terminal could be used to transfer oil from various pipelines coming from the east to an expanded Eilat-Ashqelon line. The marine terminal would thus be removed to the Mediterranean.

Several new lines or extensions of existing ones are possible, including:

I. An extension of the Yanbu' line to Aqaba
II. A direct line from Ras Tanura to Aqaba
III. A line from Kuwait to Aqaba
IV. A line linking the IPC to the Kuwait-Aqaba line
V. An extension of Tapline to Haifa

Tapline and the line from Kuwait to Aqaba can be linked; so can lines II and III. Also, the Tapline and the IPC and the proposed Iraqi-Aqaba line can be linked at their intersection, but then we strongly suggest to scrap the latter. We do, however, favor maintaining part of it and linking it with the Tapline extension to Haifa.

The Eilat-Ashqelon line should be expanded to carry 60–70 million tons a year. We suggest removing the oil port from the Eilat beach area (though this would require modifying the Israeli-Egyptian agreements on oil supplies). The line might carry 10 million tons to Ashqelon and 50 million to an oil port to be built in the Gaza Strip. The Haifa refineries would be supplied from the expanded Tapline or IPC line. The Ashdod refineries might be fed from the Eilat-Ashqelon line, but most of the crude oil passing through the system should be exported as crude, mainly to southern Europe. Together, Haifa, Ashqelon, and Gaza would export 70–80 million tons a year. This represents no more than 40 percent of Europe's oil imports from the Middle East. There are no a priori reasons for these ports not to export to the United States as well, but this question requires further study.

Each of these projects might be taken in hand in a variety of locations and on varying scales. What they have in common is that they require a relatively small investment of $50–$200 million (the Gulf-Gaza pipeline is an exception). All of them might prove attractive to foreign capital, provided trained experts and a skilled labor force are available on the spot. Obviously, before being launched, the common practice of conducting an economic analysis, including estimates of likely returns, should be followed, so as to ensure that only viable projects will be carried out.

PUBLIC SECTOR PROJECTS

There are several criteria to determine what kind of projects should be undertaken by the private sector and which should be left to the public sector. The most important, indeed the classic one, is to look at whether they provide private or public goods and services. Others are the presence of external factors with which the private sector cannot cope; overriding national objectives and policies specifically designed to meet them; requirements to make certain exceptions, which would entail changing laws and revising international agreements; and, finally, the scale of the project: the magnitude of the required investment, the length of the payoff period, and the risks involved. Traditionally, public sector projects are related to the infrastructure; in the Middle East, that means water, energy, transportation, and health. Those that are listed below are presented only by their names, which to those familiar with the Middle East mean a lot. Those who are not familiar with that region should consult other publications; for water projects, for example, see Ben-Shahar, Fishelson, and Hirsch.[6]

As for water, the following come to mind:

- the Yarmuk water storage project
- the Litani water project
- a water conduit from the Nile to northern Sinai, Gaza, and Israel
- a water supply system from the Ghor canal to the western side of the Jordan River
- a cloud-seeding project
- a joint Israeli-Egyptian power plant and water desalination facility located on the common border
- a water conveyance system to link Turkey, Israel, the West Bank and Gaza, and Jordan (and possibly Syria)

These projects require bilateral cooperation agreements—with one side, in each case, being Israel. Each will contribute to solving the water shortage problem in the areas east and west of the Jordan River, and to some extent in southern Syria and northern Sinai as well. Water shortages and their inevitable concomitant, namely, the need to allocate a very scarce resource to different political entities each claiming exclusive ownership, are thought of as a principal issue obstructing peace. Projects like those listed above would at least partially eliminate this obstacle and thereby make for a more stable and more durable peace. On a regional scale, benefits would accrue from equalizing the marginal value of water between various areas, and from generating new sources of income by means of newly available quantities of water.

This leads us to suggest the establishment of a Middle East Regional Water Authority (MERWA). To illustrate how decisively MERWA could act, let us look at the possibility of Turkey becoming the water supplier for Cyprus, Israel, Gaza, and the West Bank. There could either be a pipeline running through Syria (perhaps with various points designed for Syria to draw off water), or else water could be transported by sea, in floating balloons towed by barges. The origin of the water to be supplied would be determined according to the mode of conveyance chosen. If by pipeline, it would probably come from eastern Turkey; if by sea, or by a pipeline close to the eastern shore of the Mediterranean, it would probably come from southwest Turkey. Currently, the marginal value of the surplus water is close to zero, with the water going down into the Mediterranean or the Persian Gulf. That Turkey would have to be paid for the water goes without saying; the question is: how much. In our view, the price should not be set by individual negotiations between Turkey and the recipients, but rather by MERWA. So would the amount of royalties due to Syria for letting the pipeline cross its territory, and the price of water Syria would draw from it for itself.

MERWA might also negotiate the loans necessary to lay the pipeline or to develop the floating balloons. It should not, however, interfere in setting the price (or subsidies) for internal users of the water, whether in agriculture or in any other economic sector.

We would expect MERWA to operate in much the same way as did the European Coal and Steel Board beginning in 1953. Water in the Middle East, as an overall economic issue, is at least of the same order of magnitude as coal and steel are in Western Europe. Setting up MERWA would thus be the first step toward forming a Middle Eastern common market. Given the unique role of water in the region, if the sides succeed in cooperating in its efficient allocation, cooperation in additional areas would become comparatively easy. Next in line would be trade, tourism, communications, health, etc.

In view of the trend toward privatization, one might question why we propose a public authority rather than a private company to deal with water supply (e.g., a Middle East Water Transport, Inc.—MEWTI). MEWTI would be privately owned, by individuals or corporations, and its stock and bonds would be traded at one or more stock exchanges. It might be registered in a country outside the Middle East. In principle, this would be feasible, but there are some major disadvantages in having a private company serve as a regional authority.

First, there would be a need for a great deal of preparatory political groundwork involving leaders from the Middle East and elsewhere. Middle Eastern heads of state would want a say in forming and operating the authority. Furthermore, as noted above, the authority would be thought of as a stepping stone toward broader Middle Eastern economic cooperation, and the involvement of government leaders would continue to be necessary to bring this about. Second, as a partnership of Middle Eastern countries, MERWA would be eligible for concession loans from international institutions.

On the other hand, once MERWA is formed and once it has completed the basic framework for a regional water supply scheme, the rest could then be handled by private companies. This would be true of the detailed engineering, the construction work, and the actual operating of the scheme. We expect large international companies to compete for the contracts in question. Possibly, several Middle Eastern companies might merge to form larger, local corporations—one for each project. The actual work of erecting and operating the projects should be left to private companies, for reasons of efficiency and to avoid bureaucratic decisionmaking. The relations between MERWA and the private operating companies would have to be determined at the proper time, depending, among other things, on the legal status of MERWA.

Within the category of energy projects, the following are worth mentioning: (a) linking the electricity grids of Egypt, Israel, Jordan, and Lebanon (and perhaps Syria); (b) setting up a joint Israeli-Lebanese hydroelectric plant; and (c) creating a Red Sea—Dead Sea water canal, serving the hydroelectric and desalination plants that would be placed along it.

These energy projects would improve energy usage and production efficiency and would take advantage of natural conditions and resources to give the economies involved more, and more easily available, energy. The benefits are obvious, although the calculations for some of them are complex, for instance with regard to peak shaving in one country owing to electricity supplies coming in from another. As with water, one should start thinking about a regional energy authority that might eventually be merged with MERWA into a wider authority designed to coordinate the usage and production of both water and energy.

Transportation projects—a classic area of infrastructure activity—should deal with the region's road, rail, air, and sea transport. All these transportation projects require heavy investments, both in improving the existing underdeveloped facilities and in erecting new ones. The main benefits would be in the saving of both time and money, e.g., the cost of moving goods from one place to another in the region, or in importing or exporting goods to and from outside it. Transportation projects would facilitate the growth of internal and external trade and tourism. It is possible to identify some projects as particularly urgent, e.g., a railway from Egypt through Israel to Lebanon, Syria, Turkey, and Europe; or a highway from Iraq or the Persian Gulf to a Mediterranean port. The latter could be built running parallel to the Gulf-Gaza oil pipeline. The two projects might bring life (e.g., desert tourism) to areas now underdeveloped despite their significant economic potential.

Another example of possible cooperation in transportation is the construction of an international airport serving both Aqaba and Eilat, as well as the entire Red Sea riviera and the free tourism zone to be established along the Gulf of Aqaba. The riviera project might require the removal of Eilat's present commercial port; there is, however, nothing wrong with the idea of an Aqaba port serving Israel. Another idea is that of a joint port, a so-called Canal Port, on the common Jordanian-Israeli border, some twelve kilometers inland from Eilat. It would serve the two adjacent countries, and others as well, through the new Middle Eastern land transportation facilities to be built and interlinked (the Persian Gulf–Gaza Highway and the planned Israeli railroad to Eilat that might be extended to Egypt at one end and to Lebanon at the other). The new port would also be capable of serving as the main port of entry for Japanese goods on their way to Europe.

A regional medical center would depend, first of all, on an agreement between the public sectors of the sides involved on how to cover patient costs. Once such an agreement is reached, a regional medical center could be set up (e.g., located in Ramallah) to serve lower-level local hospitals in all the countries in the region. There is also room for thought about a regional health authority for financing research on health-related subjects specific to the Middle East and for setting priorities in public health projects for the region as a whole.

Finally, let us mention cooperation in the utilization of "nontraditional resources": climate, landscape, health-related minerals (the Dead Sea), tourist resorts (the Gulf of Eilat-Aqaba), archaeological-historical sites, and the religious sites of the area that are significant to hundreds of millions. The main economic potential is in cooperation in tourism. Fortunately, cooperation in this activity does not require heavy investments in joint projects. It requires goodwill, the removal of constraints and barriers, and organizational cooperation. The benefits would be realized by all Middle Eastern countries from upper and lower Egypt to northern Iraq (Mesopotamia).

CONCLUSIONS

Infrastructure projects move slowly and ponderously: they require huge investments (billions of dollars) and a long time to build. Even if one picks only a few of those listed above—selecting them in each category according to the lowest cost—one quickly reaches investment requirements of some $20 billion. It is a characteristic common to nearly all of them that they are capital intensive, and capital is presently a scarce resource in the region.

In a detailed study, it would be possible to assess the number of people likely to find employment—first in constructing, then in operating the schemes of each project. In most of the public projects listed above, the capital-labor ratio is likely to be above $100,000. The capital-output ratio (where it can be calculated) would be four or five to one. Hence, these projects are capital intensive, and, again, capital is a scarce resource in most Middle Eastern countries. The relatively abandoned resource is labor. For the infrastructure projects (e.g., transportation and the Yarmouk water project), only cost effectiveness can be assessed. The projects that pass the test are still very costly. Thus, once peace arrives and the region is ripe for cooperation, detailed studies are needed to assign weights to the employment benefits versus the capital requirements for each project.

Taking note of what I have said so far, it becomes clear that questions regarding the quantitative impact of the regional projects on the Middle Eastern economy as a whole can hardly be answered. All one can do is indicate orders of magnitude. Under improved economic structures and political conditions, the growth rate of per capita products in the region would be around 2–3 percent, even without the proposed regional projects being undertaken. The latter would add 1–2 percent during the construction period and another 2–3 percent when operating. This may not seem like much, but it would double the growth rate recorded for 1977–1987.

It is hardly conceivable that the regional countries will be able, in the foreseeable future, to overcome the obstacles that now prevent advanced economic cooperation and the setting up of the joint institutions necessary for such cooperation. Close, overall integration thus seems infeasible at the present time. But more modest schemes of cooperation hold out a promise of substantial economic benefits in the medium term and a prospect of underpinning peace by at least the rudiments of a closely meshed, regionwide economic network.

NOTES

1. H. Ben-Shahar, G. Fishelson, and S. Hirsch, *Economic Cooperation and Middle East Peace* (London: Weidenfeld & Nicolson, 1989).
2. Ibid., pp. 95–104.
3. Ibid., pp. 191–200.
4. Ibid., pp. 203–224.
5. Ibid., pp. 252–263.
6. Ibid., Chapter 3.

10

Areas of Potential Economic Cooperation in the Context of the Middle East Peace Process

JAWAD ANANI

This chapter presents rough proposals for achieving economic cooperation in the context of a negotiated peace process in the Middle East. The three major areas discussed here are water, job-creating investments, and financial cooperation. The choice of these three areas has been made for purposes of comprehensibility, with water a proxy for major natural resource constraints, investment covering the need of the Middle East to develop its own competitiveness and regional interdependence, and finance as the most important resource and precondition for carrying out a meaningful economic cooperation package.

Economic cooperation is assumed here to be exogenously determined by the continuity of the peace process and dialogue among the contenders. However, scoring agreements on the economic cooperation side can lubricate the hard-core political negotiation, but agreements on economics do not determine the progress of political negotiations. In other words, agreement on political terms shall dominate the potential success on the economic front.

Economic cooperation itself could be viewed as a protracted dynamic process that is not limited to a given subgeographical configuration of the Middle East. In the early stages, emphasis should be put on Israel and its contact neighbors or those with whom it already has, for whatever circumstances, an ongoing economic relationship. This relationship now has to be recognized, redefined, and redirected to achieve certain targets that would deepen the peace process. It is perhaps most expedient to deal resiliently with variously narrower or wider concepts of subregional economic cooperation, in which a regional matrix can be developed according to different but closely related scenarios of cooperation.

WATER

No subject has received attention more than water. In the absence of a regional accord, water is a serious threat to the peace and security of the Middle East; yet, the terrain through which the Jordan River and its tributaries flow is the most water-poor region. Thus, immediate attention must be given to this particular area. Yet, one must admit that the case of Syria may be singled out as the most trouble-free. However, Jordan, Lebanon, and Palestine have bilateral water issues to resolve with Israel. Therefore, we cannot talk about further cooperation before resolving the outstanding issues. The most important issues to resolve are:

1. The Wahdah Dam project on the Yarmuk River.
2. The Litani and Dao water in Lebanon.
3. The water beds and aquifers that extend into Palestinian and Israeli territories.

The water map has been totally confused since 1967, and a totally new sharing procedure must be developed. The immediate result of such a step may cause water supply stagnation in certain Israeli territories and settlements. Thus, a "transitional plan" should be devised. Of course, one could imagine some sort of a "water clearinghouse" arrangement that would accommodate the water needs of each party as a result of changing the current de facto arrangements.

The second phase in water cooperation must deal with the current regime of water uses. Agriculture seems to be the largest water guzzler, and in most cases water has sold to foreigners at highly subsidized prices. It is therefore essential that an agreement on a water-pricing mechanism be reached in order to stop the current distortion in water uses. The importance of such a price agreement is that it will stop the current injurious competition that overuses the joint water beds and aquifers in order to arrive at a new status quo.

The third phase of water cooperation should move into enhancing water sources. The feasible ambitious projects have already been discussed in more than one forum. Those proposals that make good sense are: (1) desalination projects (the Red-Dead canal); (2) the Peace Pipe involving a larger Middle East zone; (3) other water pipe projects from the Euphrates or the Nile, which are fraught with problems of their own. Here we must separate myth from reality and concentrate on feasible projects. The long-run arrangement should not exclude the idea of a prestigious regional water research center, which would invite top-notch scientists to look into water issues and come up with mutually beneficial solutions.

INVESTMENTS

It must be agreed at the outset that the absence of stability has been directly contributing to the low level of foreign investments in the region. Two major factors that must be reckoned with are poor investment laws and improper handling and treatment of foreign capital. Most of the foreign investments that have managed to gain a foothold in the Middle East have been motivated by ad hoc windfall gains or by emotional affinity with one country or another. For both the Arab countries neighboring Israel and Israel itself, the advent of peace would create a new opportunity for foreign investments to come in, whether from within the larger Middle East region itself or from overseas. The economies of Israel and its five immediate neighbors suffer from unemployment, sluggish economic growth, and balance of payments problems. They can either pursue "each on his own" policies or opt for joint efforts in certain areas of common interest. In certain cases, they may even stand to benefit from one another rather than rely on third parties. However, there are areas where some sort of cooperation already exists and can be built on.

Tourism does not have to be the source of cutthroat rivalry. On the contrary, it could benefit from the countries of the region streamlining joint ventures and granting easy access across all countries to both people and transportation media. Touristic arrangements already involve Egypt, Jordan, Palestine, and Israel. However, the current modus operandi needs restructuring on more symmetrical bases. To be specific, tourism could be regulated to give further momentum to existing programs and turn them into very profitable and job-generating operations for all the parties concerned. Even if there are reluctant parties, arrangements could be made to include at least those parties willing to engage in a given project. Thus, agreements should be reached on the following:

- Tourist transit arrangements
- Tourist pooling and financial clearing
- Regulation of touristic investments in common resource areas such as the Dead Sea, Red Sea, and holy places and shrines.

Other common areas of interest could extend to tourist-related manufacturing industries, especially those that already exist but need better marketing.

There are other areas in which joint investments can be better orchestrated. One of these areas is manufacturing and marketing agricultural produce. There is a rising international demand for goods produced in the area, such as citrus fruits, natural foods, herbs, flowers, off-season garlic and onions, and other similar products. Yet, cooperation in agriculture should be resolved first under the major heading of "water" before it can be viewed as an investment or export item.

MONEY AND FINANCE

The area of money and finance has been chosen for two main reasons. In the short run, there are numerous money matters that need to be dealt with, including many that have resulted from the Israeli occupation. In the longer term, among other considerations, the need will arise to agree on payment settlements should direct international transactions take place between some Arab countries and Israel; also to be addressed will be the need to structure a regional financial fund to help finance regional joint projects, especially those that pass the "peace criteria."

In Palestine (or occupied territories), two currencies exist, and in the future a third currency may be envisaged. Yet, the monetary behavior of Palestinians has been to use Israeli currency for daily transactions and to use Jordanian currency or the U.S. dollar as a store of value. Thus, the money supply situation is rather complex. It is further compounded by the inadequate banking facilities available in the occupied areas. In a sort of "transition period," certain arrangements must be made to stabilize the currency situation. Otherwise, chaos could prove to be painful for both Jordan and Israel. The respective central banks should find a formula of cooperation, perhaps through the International Monetary Fund (IMF), in order to arrive at a formula on how to clear the market, determine an exchange rate regime, and allow the banking system to assume the full role of a money creator. The licensing of banks, branching, supervision, and the operation of other financial intermediaries need to be watched in the "interim periods." Therefore, the establishment of an ad hoc committee representing Jordan, Palestine, and Israel, in cooperation with the IMF, to resolve such matters could prove to be important for economic stability.

It is understood that economic normalization is to go hand in hand with the political resolution of the pending issues. However, this simultaneity issue is still vague and lends itself to a variety of interpretations. For example, it is not quite clear what is meant by "economic normalization" and what the common denominators of such a process are. Yet, it is understood that more direct and face-to-face relations are expected to ensue. If this general and minimal supposition is acceptable, then the economic cooperation areas proposed thus far could acquire a minimum feasibility on the settlement of financial matters. If real transactions are to flow in one direction, it goes without saying that opposite cash flows should occur. How are these going to be organized? One option is to accept the dictates of the international monetary system. Granted, but the parties concerned should come to agree on that. The issue is easy to tackle once it is agreed upon.

It is proposed here that a Middle East bank for reconstruction and development be established. The proposed capital of the bank should be $15 billion, and it should have easy access to financial markets. It can offer direct financing to joint projects, especially those projects that cement the peace process, or it may act as a guarantor and procurer of funds. The rationale and operations of this proposed bank are similar to the recently established European bank for reconstruction and development. The question that would arise is: Who are the parties willing to take equity in the bank? It is presumptuous at this stage to call the shares, but it is reasonable to mention the potential shareholders. These are the Arab members of the Gulf Cooperation Council, the government of the United States, the European Community, the government of Japan, members of the Organization for Economic Cooperation and Development (OECD), and the beneficiaries themselves. The bank can be headquartered in the region (preferably Amman, Jordan, for many reasons), and it can give out direct loans, guarantees, and trade financing; it may engage in different types of loan terms depending on the priorities set by the board of governors. The bank may replenish its resources from the international market or by issuing bonds to certain creditors, and it may also restructure its capital every five years.

SUMMARY

In this chapter I have reviewed three potential areas of cooperation:

1. *Water,* where (a) an interim agreement is urgently needed on existing water sources and water clearing arrangements; (b) pricing policies should take precedent over any other issue among countries sharing the Jordan River and its tributaries; (c) pending issues such as dams over Yarmuk should be finalized; and (d) long-term projects such as desalination must be considered.

2. *Investments,* where emphasis is laid on tourism as a job-creating activity, which could be done in a highly coordinated fashion with little political friction. A special ad hoc committee is needed to iron out difficulties facing the cross-border movement of people and vehicles. Other issues related to pooling, investments, and coordination in joint touristic facilities can also be pursued.

3. *Money and banking,* where interim arrangements are needed to cope with the existing multicurrency system in the occupied territories. A joint committee, including the IMF, should meet to oversee and facilitate the transition. In the longer run, a Middle East bank for reconstruction and development is proposed.

PART III

THE POTENTIAL FOR ARMS CONTROL IN THE MIDDLE EAST

11

Middle East Security and Arms Control

MARK A. HELLER

The purpose of this chapter is to assess the parameters of the military component of the Middle Eastern security agenda, broadly defined, and to suggest some guiding principles of cooperative security in the Middle East. The analysis focuses on three basic principles—linkages, asymmetries, and intermediate measures—whose recognition and acceptance appear to be essential if constructive debate and productive negotiations are to take place.

"Cooperative security" is, at best, a nebulous idea and, at worst, a faddish slogan. Other qualifiers have been used to describe various types of security situations or policies, but "cooperative security," though widely employed, is of too recent origin to have acquired a conventional definition.[1] Insofar as the military dimension is concerned, however, it would seem to imply the codification of measures and the development of multilateral institutions to enhance the security of all parties in a systemic conflict relationship by reducing the threat that military force will be used offensively in pursuit of political objectives, i.e., that it will be an instrument of political/strategic (as opposed to tactical/operational) doctrine. Cooperative security therefore presupposes not the absence of conflictual relations or disputed objectives, but rather the renunciation of the first use of force to promote political aims, prosecute conflicts, or resolve disputes.

Specific measures and institutions associated with cooperative security derive logically from basic foreign and national security policy concerning the use of force. Their purpose should be to confer credibility on the policy; to create confidence in the sincerity of the commitment to it; and to reduce ambiguities, misunderstandings, misperceptions, or defects in control systems that lead to accidental or inadvertent attack or preemption unwarranted by the real intentions of the adversary.

Renunciation of the first use of force makes it possible to contemplate changes in orders of battle, force postures, and military doctrines and to discuss various types of arms control agreements and confidence- and security-building measures (CSBMs) that reduce one side's capability for and the other side's fear of offensive military action. However, when war is retained as a policy option because of intense dissatisfaction with the status quo or some other political imperative, there will be far less willingness to endorse the measures and institutions associated with cooperative security, i.e., less willingness to constrain one's own offensive capabilities even in return for similar constraints on the other side.

It is therefore not surprising that in the Middle East, systematic thinking about arms control and other elements of cooperative security has begun to take place only in Israel and Egypt, the only country in a state of peace with Israel.[2] With respect to the rest of the region, the idea that serious arms control or CSBMs could be implemented—except for the imposed and extremely intrusive version applied to Iraq under the terms of UN Security Council Resolution 687—is often depicted as naive, or at best premature. The same approach seems to prevail in other regions of the world marked by protracted political and/or primordial conflict, e.g., South Asia and the Korean peninsula, where there is also considerable skepticism (mixed with hopeful analysis) about the applicability of arms control and security-building concepts and models drawn primarily from the European/East-West experience.[3]

LINKAGES

The first guiding principle must therefore be recognition that while arms control and other elements of cooperative security may be conceptually distinct from the state of political relations between adversaries, they are practically linked in the most intimate way. Arms control cannot be simply a technical exercise carried out in a political vacuum. Nor can it be a substitute for the resolution of political disputes. The pursuit of an ambitious system of cooperative security makes sense only when there is mutual recognition of the right to security, that is, when political relations among all parties no longer imply a state of war in which the threat or use of military force to challenge the status quo is retained as a viable policy option. This should be obvious from the history of East-West arms control and cooperative security relations, which were marked by painfully slow progress and were frequently stalled or derailed by political tensions long after either side abandoned any intention of going to war against the other to promote its objectives (if, indeed, such an intention ever existed).

In the Arab-Israeli context, this means that a comprehensive cooperative security regime—with a European-type plethora of conferences, institutions, arms control agreements, and intensive and intrusive interactions—can only be instituted as part of a general settlement of outstanding political conflicts, primarily (though not exclusively) the Israeli-Palestinian and Israeli-Syrian conflicts. Indeed, such a regime can hardly be conceived, much less negotiated, unless there is simultaneous movement toward a general settlement, and a sense that the end of the state of war is either in hand or clearly in view.

At the same time, however, security concerns, especially of Israel, are themselves major factors in the political process, and unless these concerns are also addressed and satisfied, it is virtually certain that the political obstacle to ending the state of war—Arab rejection of the status quo—will not be removed and the fundamental precondition of cooperative security will not be met. At the level of abstract logic, this is not a "chicken-and-egg" problem, since a basic political determination with respect to the use of force must precede the adoption of real cooperative security measures. In practice, however, the changes (or "progress") at both levels will be incremental and synergistic, in the sense that limited military/technical confidence-building measures can reduce the insecurities associated with commitments needed to change the political relationship in ways that would permit a more far-reaching cooperative security regime. In short, political relations of coexistence and the military dimensions of cooperative security are mutually contingent and mutually reinforcing, and need to be pursued simultaneously.

ASYMMETRIES

Implicit in the logic of linkages is a second principle, that of asymmetries in weapons or force limitations. If the purpose of arms control and other co-operative security measures is to reduce instabilities and uncertainties, to minimize the risk of accidental or inadvertent war, and especially to enhance confidence that adversaries will not be able to mount an effective surprise attack even if they are inclined to try despite political commitments, it is important that these measures not be based on formulas of ostensibly equal limitations that simply perpetuate unstable asymmetries at lower quantitative levels. Instead, cooperative security arrangements must acknowledge the different needs and concerns of the various actors resulting from situational asymmetries—of geography, human and other resources, alliance possibilities, doctrine, force postures, and orders-of-battle—and incorporate the principle that unequal restrictions are needed to compensate for instabilities inherent in these asymmetries. CFE (Conventional Forces in Europe) negotiations in Europe took account of this requirement by focusing on and providing for asymmetrical cuts of those components of forces that were most suited for surprise, offensive operations, such as Soviet tank armies.

In the Middle East, the logic of asymmetries is even stronger because cooperative security measures will presumably be implemented, not on the basis of the territorial status quo, as was the case in Europe, but rather in the context of a political settlement that at some stage and to some extent leads to reduced Israeli control of important geomilitary assets in the West Bank and Golan Heights. In other words, the linkage between politics and cooperative security entails asymmetrical security risks for Israel, and these also must find expression in asymmetrical arms control measures.

The specific asymmetrical limitations required by a comprehensive cooperative security regime in the Middle East are numerous, and the following examples are intended simply to illustrate the kinds of measures that could enhance security by reducing asymmetries in offensive conventional capabilities:

1. Any territories relinquished by Israel in the context of a settlement must be governed by some combination of Israeli military presence, maintenance of early-warning facilities, and exclusion of Arab forces.

2. Any other geographical limitations on force deployments may be mutual, but they must in practice be unequal to reflect the lack of geographical depth in Israel (this principle was incorporated in the limitation-of-forces provisions of the Egyptian-Israeli peace treaty).

3. Some proportion of Arab ground formations should be permanently converted from standing to reserve forces, to reduce the possibility of short-warning attack. Asymmetries, of course, imply certain trade-offs between various components of the military dimension. Even in ostensibly cooperative or "positive-sum" arrangements, adversaries will inevitably attempt to maximize their own advantage and to achieve arms control limitations that constrain the other side more, at least in a relative sense, by emphasizing those elements that play a more important role in the other side's doctrine, force structure, or overall capability. It is unlikely that Arab parties will agree to asymmetrical limitations that address Israeli concerns, even in the conventional realm, without at least trying to secure some corresponding reassurances concerning asymmetries, especially qualitative (e.g., in training, technical expertise, intelligence, leadership, indigenous production, and/or modification capabilities), that favor Israel. Because of their more nebulous character, these advantages will be difficult to translate into negotiable currency, but because they result in certain tactical and operational superiorities, they will somehow need to be expressed in discussions about asymmetrical trade-offs.

Beyond the conventional field, asymmetrical trade-offs will have to deal with different types of unconventional weapons and also bridge the distinction between the two categories. In recent years, for example, Arab states have deflected efforts to constrain the development, procurement, and stockpiling of chemical weapons, arguing that such weapons are necessary to balance Israel's presumed superiority in nuclear weapons and that the focus of efforts should therefore be broadened to encompass all weapons of mass destruction. But if chemical weapons could serve as a counterdeterrent to Israel's nuclear deterrent, they would revive the salience of Arab quantitative superiority in conventional forces. The differential importance attributed to different types of weapons means that linkages between conventional and unconventional weapons and forces, as well as between various types of unconventional weapons, will therefore be necessary if any significant limitations are to be achieved.

INTERMEDIATE MEASURES

If a comprehensive cooperative security regime is predicated on the achievement of a truly peaceful Middle East, then the idea of such a regime may very well be utopian. For the obstacles to a general settlement and stable regional peace are truly enormous. A comprehensive and definitive Israeli-Arab peace agreement, however improbable, is merely a necessary condition for general stability; it is far from sufficient. Other requirements include stable and moderate representative governments throughout the region; equitable distribution of wealth within and among the various states of the region in its broadest sense; structural solutions to economic, resource, and demographic problems; creation of a political formula to accommodate ethnic and religious heterogeneity; the preempting or discrediting of the appeal of millennial religio-national or political movements and ideologies within and around the region (including the Muslim-populated areas of the former Soviet Union); stability in the world oil market; and effective conflict prevention and resolution actions by outside powers and international institutions.[4]

Given the formidable nature of these conditions, it is reasonable to conclude that a comprehensive cooperative regime for the Middle East is a very remote and perhaps completely fanciful prospect. Even if this is true, however, it does not warrant the belief that nothing at all can be done in advance of a truly stable, general peace. That would be the counsel of despair, what has sometimes been referred to as "paralysis by analysis." Moreover, it would be empirically unfounded. The history of the Arab-Israeli conflict is studded with arms control and confidence-building measures of various sorts, especially disengagement-of-forces, demilitarization, and limitation-of-forces agreements and military-to-military contacts in mixed armistice commissions. These precedents, of course, are very modest and context-specific, the practical outcome of mutual agreements to end a particular phase of fighting. Nevertheless, they indicate that some minimal common interests can exist even in a continuing state of war.

Even parties that have not renounced the war option as a matter of basic policy are concerned about inadvertent or accidental war, i.e., the possibility that war could begin at a time or in circumstances not of their own choosing. Nor can most of the parties be indifferent or immune to the economic consequences of unrestrained arms races. Some beneficiaries of foreign assistance have already been adversely affected by the collapse of Soviet power, and others are likely to feel the impact of U.S. unwillingness or inability to continue bearing the costs of large-scale aid programs in the future. Furthermore, several countries face unique economic challenges, such as the massive Soviet Jewish immigration to Israel and the huge influx of indigent Palestinians to Jordan, which will make it even harder to sustain the burden of arms races. Only Saudi Arabia, Iran, and some of the smaller oil-exporting sheikhdoms in the Gulf are able fairly easily to finance continuing military buildups, and even they are exposed to the vagaries of the oil market and urgent demands for alternative uses.

All of this suggests that some sorts of minor confidence-building and arms control measures are possible in advance of major breakthroughs on the central political, economic, and social questions. Furthermore, such measures are necessary, given the political-military linkage, if the psychological environment for more ambitious negotiations is ever to be created. Of course, the existing climate of conflict and distrust means that some of the measures familiar from the East-West or European experience, such as hotline agreements and risk-reduction centers, are unlikely to be helpful even if they were feasible. Prenotification of large-scale military maneuvers, for example, would probably be viewed as a trick rather than a measure of reassurance, more likely to raise tension than to lower it. Nevertheless, it is possible to imagine some minor, essentially unilateral measures that could have a confidence-building effect; one example that springs to mind is restricting training flights or missile tests to nonthreatening trajectories.

In the present circumstances, however, the most promising possibilities are reserved to third parties. Pending a decision by the protagonists themselves to institute political relations compatible with cooperative security agreements, outside actors can have at least a modest impact on crisis behavior in the region and on Middle Eastern arms races. In the first area, third parties, especially the United States, can help reduce uncertainties by increasing the information available to local actors about adversary actions, especially about potentially destabilizing troop movements, mobilizations, or other apparent preparations for war. This implies intelligence sharing, although it should be recognized that information from third parties would not necessarily be viewed as more trustworthy, reliable, or devoid of conscious distortion for political reasons than would information supplied by an adversary. The greatest contribution to transparency would therefore be the provision of equipment that would give local actors direct access to real-time information from third-party technical means, especially U.S. satellites. Outside actors could also help to reduce the risks of breakdown in command-and-control systems where defects are believed to exist, especially for destabilizing weapons such as ballistic missiles.[5] Such help could include the provision of postlaunch command-destruct systems and other control technologies.

Finally, outside parties can act much more vigorously on the question of supply-side arms control. Much thought has been given to this issue, but there has been no real suppliers' regime since the tripartite system of the early 1950s, no effective partial controls despite NPT (Non-Proliferation Treaty), MTCR (Missile Technology Control Regime), the Australia Group, and other mechanisms, and no serious effort to address the question of conventional arms transfers since the Soviet-U.S. talks in the late 1970s.

Not all types of weapons proliferation are equally threatening; not all states (or, to be more precise, regimes) are equally opposed to the status quo. Logically, therefore, supply-side control should be selective, targeting first the most destabilizing weapons systems and the major centers of regional instability, i.e., those actors most likely to use force in pursuit of revisionist political objectives. In some cases, this logic leads to proposals based on functional selectivity, such as a moratorium on surface-to-surface missile transfers and tightened export controls on technologies and materials geared to weapons of mass destruction.[6] In other instances, what is advocated is geographical selectivity, such as the demand, not only that the prohibition on all transfers of military and dual-use technologies to Iraq be maintained, but also that it be extended to Libya, Iran, and Syria, as well.[7]

However, effective supply-side controls would require more than coordination among the leading Western exporters—the United States, Britain, and France—and the strict enforcement of laws regulating the activities of private companies in other countries such as Germany and Italy. They would also have to enlist the cooperation of the major non-Western suppliers (especially China and Russia), who, if nothing else, remain an important factor in the Middle Eastern arms market. And there is nothing to suggest why all these suppliers (not to speak of other exporters to the region) will be better able in the future to agree on precisely how such a selective regime should be implemented, i.e., to reach a universally accepted definition of the relative sources of instability or of the most destabilizing weapons, than they have been in the past. To cite only one example, Chinese spokespersons have argued that China is simply being discriminated against by other suppliers who demand controls on transfers of ballistic missile technology (in which China has made a special investment and achieved something of a comparative advantage) while refusing to do anything about the huge volume of conventional arms sales (including such delivery systems as long-range artillery, rockets, and strike aircraft). The only hope (however faint) for any agreement among suppliers therefore lies in a blunt instrument that appears not to disadvantage anyone, that is, an across-the-board moratorium on all arms transfers to the entire region for at least several years, and certainly as long as there remains some hope for productive negotiations among Arabs and Israelis.

Some analysts, convinced that selective supply-side controls are not only preferable but also feasible, have rejected the idea of an indiscriminate across-the-board embargo "from Marrakesh to Bangladesh."[8] But it is precisely the indiscriminate character of such a measure that gives it any chance of being adopted by the major suppliers and of being endorsed, however reluctantly (though this matters less), by the major recipients. For in the aftermath of the Gulf War, there appear to be no military imbalances in the region of the type that create strong incentives for anyone to go to war. At the same time, however, the Middle East does seem poised on the very brink (if not already in the throes) of a major new arms race with potentially ruinous consequences for the region itself, and perhaps for others as well. A suppliers' moratorium, even if not perfectly leak-proof, would make it much more difficult for such an arms race to unfold or continue, whatever the preferences of local actors. It would also make possible significant economic savings, and, most importantly, it might produce the breathing space needed to facilitate the political progress upon which a more ambitious and effective comprehensive security regime depends.

NOTES

1. Richard Smoke, for example, confines the use of the term "mutual security" to dyadic relationships and describes a mutual security policy as "simply a policy that aims to improve the security of both sides, under conditions of some mutual insecurity." *A Theory of Mutual Security*, Working Paper no. 11 (Providence: Brown University Center for Foreign Policy Development, November 1990), p. 5. Smoke goes to some length to distinguish "mutual" from "common," "collective," and "global" security, but makes no reference to "cooperative security."

2. See, for example, Dore Gold, ed., *Arms Control in the Middle East* (Tel Aviv: Jaffee Center for Strategic Studies, 1990).

3. See "Arms Control on the Korean Peninsula," special issue of *The Korean Journal of Defense Analysis* 3, no. 1 (Summer 1991), especially Jonathan Dean, "Arms Control on the Korean Peninsula: How Is the European Experience Applicable?" pp. 67–84; and Andrew Mack, "The Theory of Non-provocative Defense: How Relevant for Korea?" pp. 241–259.

4. For a more detailed catalog of these conditions, see Anthony H. Cordesman, "Regional Security Options in the Middle East: The Politics of Reality Versus the Politics of Hope" (mimeo, July 25, 1991), pp. 6–7.

5. For more on the problems of missile proliferation and crisis stability, see Mark A. Heller, "Coping with Missile Proliferation in the Middle East," *Orbis* 35, no. 1 (Winter 1991), pp. 15–28.

6. See Geoffrey Kemp, "The Middle East Arms Race: Can It Be Controlled?" *Middle East Journal* 45, no. 3 (Summer 1991), pp. 441–456.

7. For example, Senator John McCain, "Arms Sales to the Middle East Since the Gulf War" (mimeo, November 1991).

8. Ibid., p. 1.

12

Arms Control in
the Middle East

ALAN PLATT

The full ramifications of the end of the Cold War and the aftermath of the Gulf War will not become clear for quite a long time. Inside and outside governments, in Washington and around the world, analysts are studying these developments, which took place at such dizzying speed that they outpaced the ability to comprehend them and their implications. Moreover, this assessment process will undoubtedly continue to go on for the foreseeable future.

One region of the world that is being heavily studied as part of this assessment process is the Middle East, which is now, at least from the United States' point of view, among the most likely sites of future international hostilities. In light of the Gulf War and long-standing historical rivalries in the Middle East, there is widespread concern about the past and future importation of sophisticated conventional weapons into this already heavily armed region of the world. Saddam Hussein has sent the nations of the world a wake-up call about what large quantities of highly advanced arms can lead to in the Middle East and how large inventories of conventional and unconventional arms in this region, if unchecked, can threaten global stability. Not surprisingly, there is now growing international interest in exploring arms control possibilities in the Middle East. In this chapter, I will first address the growing arms competition, a competition that threatens to pick up speed after the Gulf War across a range of conventional and unconventional weaponry. Following a discussion of the arms competition in the region, I will put forward several ideas about what might be done to help curb this competition.

Implicit in the discussion is the idea that arms inherently do not cause conflicts; wars are brought about by competing, hostile nations, and any long-term solution to conflict in the Middle East must ultimately involve the cooperation of the nations in the region. Nevertheless, a key premise of this chapter is that certain flows of arms can aggravate tensions in the Middle East and can make conflict more likely. Accordingly, it is useful and important at this time to explore the possibilities of arms control in the Middle East, and the most fruitful place to start is with initiatives from the world's major arms suppliers.

Arms control is herein thought of as "any measure that reduces the likelihood of war as an instrument of policy or that limits the destructiveness and duration of war should it break out."[1] Hence, arms control does not per se mean arms reductions or disarmament. Nor does it necessarily involve the kind of comprehensive, negotiated weapons agreements that have characterized recent U.S.-Soviet arms control efforts. As was concluded in a recent report that reflected a series of discussions about arms control among a group of Americans and representatives of different Middle Eastern countries, for the Middle East, "arms control encompasses any measure that strengthens regional stability and diminishes war as an attractive instrument of national policy whether by design or perceived necessity."[2]

Accordingly, arms control in the Middle East now holds potential promise not as an end in and of itself but rather as a means to achieving, at least initially, modest but useful objectives. This, in fact, was how arms control was most effectively pursued by the United States and the Soviet Union during much of the postwar era when serious political differences divided the two superpowers. In this light, the pursuit of arms control in the Middle East today can most usefully be compared to the pursuit of arms control between the superpowers during the 1950s, not the 1990s. Indeed, arms control has traditionally been more effective between adversaries than between allies, because its potential benefit is most obvious in adversarial circumstances and the parties' interest is correspondingly keenest. For example, arms control can prevent escalation of conflict from political miscalculation or the perception on one side that another country has acquired new, first-strike, threatening armaments. At a minimum, arms control measures could delay or possibly prevent a new round of weapons competition and military activities that, if left unchecked, could serve as a catalyst to inadvertent war (i.e., a war neither side wanted or expected at the outset of a crisis).[3]

In any case, in light of the aftermath of the Gulf War, recent important changes in Soviet foreign and defense policy, and the growing burden of high defense spending levels on a number of economies in the Middle East, now seems to be an opportune moment to try to examine the possibilities of arms control in the region. Any such efforts, moreover, can and must go forward in parallel with the peace process. To be sure, there are serious limits on what can ultimately be achieved through Middle East arms control efforts initiated by the world's leading arms-supplying nations without forward movement on some of the larger issues that divide the nations of the region. Nevertheless, it is worthwhile to consider the possibilities for arms control in the absence of such movement. Indeed, progress on the arms control front, however modest, might well have a positive impact on efforts to achieve peace in the region.

THE ARMS COMPETITION IN THE MIDDLE EAST

For military, political, cultural, and historical reasons, Middle Eastern nations have over the years pursued their national security interests primarily by expanding and modernizing their military forces, not by reaching political compromises that mutually constrain military capabilities. Accordingly, both conventional (e.g., advanced fighter aircraft, armored combat vehicles, artillery, helicopters, and tanks) and unconventional arms (e.g., ballistic missiles, chemical weapons, and biological weapons) abound in this region.

Conventional Arms

The largest suppliers of conventional arms to the Middle East as well as worldwide have been for a long time and are likely to continue to be the five permanent members of the United Nations Security Council: the United States, the former Soviet Union, France, the United Kingdom, and the People's Republic of China. As Alvin Rubinstein has summarily observed in a recent article, "From 1974 to 1989, the five permanent members of the UN Security Council accounted for more than 75 percent of the estimated total of $220 to $250 billion in arms trade in the Middle East."[4]

During most of this period, the respective market shares of the five largest arms exporters changed significantly, but the two largest suppliers were the two superpowers—the United States and the Soviet Union—which produced two out of every three weapons transferred to the Middle East during the period 1970–1990. Of the two superpowers, the Soviet Union was the leading exporter of arms to the region during most of the 1980s. However, during the past few years, the United States has significantly increased its arms exports to the Middle East, while Soviet sales declined after 1987. The most recently released official U.S. data show that the United States led the Soviet Union in Middle Eastern arms sales in 1990 for the first time in any given year since 1983, a fact reflecting the more than $14.5 billion in U.S. arms sales to Saudi Arabia in 1990.[5]

Moreover, the United States' role as the world's preeminent conventional arms supplier grew in 1991 and is likely to grow even more in coming years as a result of both the effectiveness of U.S.-made high-tech weapons in the Gulf War and the decline in the military and financial attractiveness of Soviet weapons exports. Indeed, since the Gulf War began in 1990 U.S. defense companies have signed agreements to sell more than $20 billion worth of weapons to Middle Eastern countries. Further, the pace of U.S. weapons exports seems to be accelerating: in July 1991, the Bush administration sent notifications to Congress of roughly $1.3 billion of planned U.S. military exports to Egypt, Oman, and Saudi Arabia, and there is every reason to believe that these sorts of proposed U.S. arms transfer notifications will continue for the next couple of years. At the same time, France announced a 70 percent jump in its weapons exports in 1990; the People's Republic of China continues to sell various sophisticated arms around the Middle East, and the former Soviet Union reportedly completed a $2 billion arms sale to Syria in late 1991, among other sales.[6] In addition, several other European countries—Germany, Italy, and Spain—have become significant weapons exporters to the Middle East arms market, as have a number of other less developed countries, including Argentina, Brazil, Czechoslovakia, India, and North and South Korea. And as this latter group of less developed countries increasingly seeks hard currency to fuel economic growth, it would be surprising if they did not look to arms exports to the Middle East as a major source of hard currency.[7]

Among conventional arms buyers, during the past four years, five of the world's ten largest arms recipients have been in the Middle East: Saudi Arabia has been the premier arms purchaser in the world; Iraq was second; Iran was third; Syria was eighth; and Egypt was tenth.[8] Of course, with the end of the Iran-Iraq war and the current embargo of arms to Iraq, the rank ordering of arms recipients is likely to change in coming years. However, the demand for arms in the region is likely to remain substantial, with many of the oil-rich countries in the region, led by Saudi Arabia and several of the smaller Gulf states like the United Arab Emirates, likely to increase their demand as a result of the Gulf War.

Part of this demand will be met by the world's major arms suppliers, likely led by the United States. Part of the demand will be met by those less developed countries around the world seeking to gain hard currency by building up their arms export industries. Part of the demand will also be met by growing indigenous arms capabilities. This effort among Middle Eastern countries to substitute indigenously manufactured weapons for expensive imported equipment is being driven by hopes of economic gain, feelings of national pride and sovereignty, and a desire to reduce the vulnerabilities that flow from dependence on foreign arms suppliers. Within the region, Israel and Egypt have already developed highly sophisticated arms production capabilities, and a number of other Middle Eastern countries are moving to expand their indigenous arms production capabilities.[9]

Unconventional Weapons
Given the fact that in coming years ballistic missiles are increasingly likely to carry unconventional warheads (e.g., chemical, biological, nuclear) as

compared to conventional explosives, they are included in this discussion of unconventional weapons, although the categorization is not yet uniformly accepted in the United States, among other places. At the same time as Middle East nations are rapidly acquiring sophisticated conventional arms, they are also expanding their ballistic missile capabilities. At present, eight Middle Eastern countries possess ballistic missiles—Egypt, Iran, Iraq, Israel, Libya, Saudi Arabia, Syria, and Yemen. Five of these countries have, in fact, employed missiles during recent conflicts: Syria and Egypt during the 1973 Arab-Israeli War; Iran and Iraq during their "War of the Cities" in the 1980s; Libya when it fired at least two Scud missiles against U.S. forces in retaliation for the U.S. bombing attacks against Libya in 1986; and, of course, Iraq when it fired Scud missiles at Israel and Saudi Arabia in the recent Gulf War.

These missiles and the technology for their production have come from a number of countries, including the former Soviet Union, the People's Republic of China, the United States, and North and South Korea, among others. As a result of the transfer of this technology to the region, Egypt, Iran, Iraq, Israel, and Libya now have indigenous missile programs, and Syria has developed the potential to enhance the capabilities of foreign-supplied missiles by giving them new warheads.[10]

Concurrent with the proliferation of ballistic missiles in the region is the continuing proliferation of chemical and biological weapons. The most authoritative official U.S. statement regarding the status of chemical weapons programs in the Middle East was made by Thomas Brooks, director of Naval Intelligence, in testimony given to the House Armed Services Committee in March 1991, soon after the end of the Gulf War. Brooks reaffirmed U.S. support for the Geneva Protocol of 1925, which bans the first use of chemical weapons, and reasserted U.S. interest in the early conclusion of an international agreement to ban chemical weapons. At the same time, Brooks observed that six countries in the Middle East now either have a chemical weapons capability or are in the process of acquiring one—Egypt, Iran, Iraq, Israel, Libya, and Syria.[11] Since Brooks's testimony, there has been growing speculation that Saudi Arabia is also in the process of acquiring and developing a chemical weapons capability.

According to U.S. Defense Secretary Dick Cheney, four of the Middle Eastern countries that have chemical weapons—Iran, Iraq, Libya, and Syria—have now also acquired a capability in biological weapons, i.e., living organisms that spread such diseases as anthrax and typhus.[12] It is widely believed that Egypt and Israel have also developed biological weapons capabilities in recent months, although only Syria and Iraq are thought to be capable of actually producing deliverable biological warheads. Moreover, every country believed to be developing biological weapons is also on the list of proliferating chemical weapons states. This seems to lend support to the idea that the two are related and that "prevention of chemical warfare programs provides an important—perhaps even essential—firebreak against biological weapons proliferation."[13]

What Is to Be Done?

Given the quantitative and qualitative growth of conventional arms in the Middle East, the spreading of ballistic missile technology in the region, and the continuing proliferation of chemical weapons and biological weapons, what arms control initiatives are possible to limit this weapons competition? It is hopelessly optimistic and probably wrong to assume that this competition will end soon, whether through unilateral, bilateral, or multilateral efforts. On the other hand, it is also wrong to assume that these trends are inexorable and irreversible and therefore to conclude that nothing can be done.

Initially, modest steps can and should be taken to help curb this competition. First, there should be a concerted effort among the world's leading arms suppliers to limit the quantity and quality of sophisticated conventional arms being exported to the Middle East. The Gulf War, after all, was fought with sophisticated conventional arms, as have most recent outbreaks of violence in the Middle East and elsewhere. Further, if the world's major arms suppliers are not seen to be committed de facto to arms control concerning conventional weapons, it will be hard to persuade the nations of the Middle East that arms control is to be taken seriously overall. Increased transparency and the institutionalization of a United Nations registry of arsenals and arms transfers are good first steps. But they should be understood as such: the world's five major arms suppliers involved in current multilateral talks must go beyond well-meaning rhetoric and steps to increase transparency about arms transfers.

In this regard, the United States, as the world's preeminent arms supplier, must take the lead if the effort is to be credible and meaningful. In his commencement address to the United States Air Force Academy on May 29, 1991, President Bush did in fact call for supplier guidelines on conventional weapons exports. Pursuant to this call, representatives of the United States, the People's Republic of China, France, the United Kingdom, and the former Soviet Union have officially met on several occasions. At the meeting in Paris in July 1991, it was agreed that the five permanent members of the United Nations Security Council "would not transfer weaponry in circumstances which would undermine stability." They also expressed their intention "to develop modalities of consultation and information exchanges" concerning arms transfers and observe "rules of restraint" when considering conventional weapon transfers to the Middle East, "taking into account the special situation (in the Middle East) as a primary area of tension."[14]

Nevertheless, the five permanent members of the United Nations Security Council, while holding periodic meetings on multilateral arms transfer restraint, have not yet demonstrated seriousness about implementing concrete multilateral restraint guidelines. Their near-term preference seems to favor new conventional arms transfers to support their allies' security interests in the region, accompanied by high-flown, generalized rhetoric supporting arms control. Unfortunately, this approach may well doom subsequent arms transfer restraint efforts. The world's five major arms suppliers need to take the initiative first among themselves and then among the so-called second-tier suppliers (e.g., Argentina, Brazil, Germany, India, Italy, and South Africa) to adopt a quantitative guideline stating that weapons in the five categories of equipment covered under the Conventional Forces in Europe treaty—armored combat vehicles, artillery, fighter aircraft, helicopters, and tanks—should not be transferred to the region in quantities that exceed current ceilings. One-for-one replacement of these types of weapons might initially be permitted, although actual reductions in numbers would be envisaged as individual nations modernized their existing inventories. For every system transferred to a country or developed indigenously, the recipient nation would be expected to destroy an agreed-upon comparable system.

In addition to proposing and agreeing to such a guideline—and trying to encourage regional recipient support for this effort—the five powers should adopt at least two qualitative restraint guidelines. First, certain weapons systems at the high end of the technology scale that are not currently present in the Middle East or that are in the region in only limited quantities should not be transferred to the Middle East. This guideline would ban, for example, the introduction into the region of such systems as stealth aircraft, advanced cruise missiles, and newest-generation, night vision equipment. Second, export controls should be strengthened on dual-use technologies that can radically multiply the capabilities of weapon platforms. The five powers should take the lead in developing a refocused COCOM (Coordinating Committee on Multilateral Export Controls)-type organization for the purpose of developing, monitoring, and enforcing an agreed-upon list of technologies whose transfer to the Middle East would be strictly monitored. Advanced night vision equipment, sophisticated information-processing software, and guidance technologies would be the kinds of items on this list.

In addition to developing, implementing, and enforcing conventional arms transfer restraint guidelines, the world's five major arms suppliers should give far higher priority to supporting and furthering international efforts to curb the proliferation of unconventional weapons. Concerning the proliferation of ballistic missiles, the Missile Technology Control Regime (MTCR), which was established in 1987 by Canada, France, Germany, Italy, Japan, the United Kingdom, and the United States, has worked relatively well given its limited membership, scope, and mandate. It has, for example, retarded the international sale of space-launched vehicles and ballistic missiles with a range of more than 300 kilometers. Among its now seventeen signatories, it has also provided for stricter review procedures for such dual-use components as rocket casings and staging technologies to prevent their use in the development of ballistic missile programs. However, a number of key potential exporters of missile technology remain outside the MTCR, including Argentina, Brazil, China, India, and North and South Korea (the former Soviet Union has not formally signed the agreement but has adhered to the strictures of the MTCR). In the future, the United States should strive to expand membership in the MTCR, ensure that its guidelines are taken seriously by the signatories, and strongly enhance its enforceability. Moreover, the five powers should go beyond merely extending the MTCR and should call for a freeze on the procurement and testing of these systems in the Middle East. They should also push to curtail their proliferation through a ban on the sale of missiles or their component technologies by all suppliers to Middle Eastern countries.

Concerning chemical weapons, the Australia Group, an informal grouping of twenty industrialized nations plus the European Community represented as such, has been relatively successful since January 1987 in coming up with a list of chemical precursors most important to the development of chemical weapons. This list of precursors is now governed by a set of export control regulations established by the Group. In an agreement reached in Paris in the spring of 1991, the member nations of the Australia Group agreed to go further and require private companies to obtain licenses before exporting any of the fifty chemical precursors to nations other than those that are part of the Group. No Middle Eastern countries, however, are part of the Australia Group at this time.

In the future, the United States must give the conclusion of a Chemical Weapons Convention much higher priority than it has received thus far. For only with a push from the world's major arms suppliers, starting with the United States, will this convention be completed soon and contain the kind of managed inspection procedures that will make circumvention difficult. High-level efforts among the world's major arms suppliers also need to be increasingly focused on putting effective verification provisions into the 132-member 1972 Biological Weapons Convention. Concerning both chemical and biological weapons, such international arms control efforts will work only if they are accorded the highest priority in practice by world leaders and include some related confidence- and security-building measures, intrusive verification measures to detect would-be violators, and tight, coordinated economic sanctions to punish violating countries.[15]

Besides expanding their efforts to make these international arms control efforts more meaningful and widely accepted in the Middle East, the world's major arms suppliers need to help develop a series of confidence- and security-building measures that would be relevant to and potentially acceptable to the countries in the Middle East. In the European area, two general but different approaches to arms control were pursued in the 1970s and 1980s. One effort, called the structural approach, centered on international negotiations in Vienna, where NATO and the Warsaw Pact had been engaged in the Mutual and Balanced Force Reduction (MBFR) talks since 1973. These negotiations focused on reducing the numbers of military forces stationed on the Central European front. These talks concentrated on scaling down the two blocs' personnel, units, and military equipment. The second approach focused not on the structure of forces but on their operation and has been referred to as the "operational" approach to arms control.[16] With antecedents in the Helsinki Final Act of 1975, the operational approach culminated in September 1986, after three years of negotiations, in the Document of the Stockholm Conference on Confidence and Security-Building Measures (CSBM). That document lays out various agreed-upon regulations governing the two blocs' military activities in Europe: forecasting in advance or otherwise announcing exercises or concentrations of troops in excess of various thresholds, inviting observers to such activities, and setting out procedures for inspections of questionable activities.

While such confidence- and security-building measures may be hard to achieve in the Middle East in the near term (it was eleven years from the Helsinki Final Act to the Stockholm accords), they are likely to have more relevance and utility in the Middle East than the structural approach for the foreseeable future. Confidence-building measures, exploratory and experimental by nature, can start at a relatively trivial level, such as expanding the exchange of routine information, arranging soccer games among military units, or holding seminars on nonmilitary regional issues (e.g., the environment). In due course, they could incrementally move to the area of transparency, i.e., less secrecy about military activities. This was the area where progress was first made in Europe in 1975, with relatively simple procedures for announcing certain military exercises. Such efforts have the potential to be highly useful to all the parties in the region. As James Goodby, former U.S. ambassador to the Conference on Security and Cooperation in Europe negotiations on CSBMs, has observed:

> What transparency usually can offer is freedom from fear—fear caused by unfounded worries about surprise attack and fear driven by exaggerated estimates of an adversary's equipment holdings. Conversely, transparency can also confirm that fears are truly justified and in such instances, transparency offers warning time during which governments can act, either by mobilizing forces or by redressing an equipment imbalance.[17]

Historically, confidence-building measures involving increased transparency have advanced incrementally to ever more serious and important levels. Beyond increased information exchange, substantive confidence-building measures that ultimately should be considered in the Middle East context include: hotline agreements, either bilateral or multilateral through an agreed-upon third party; the expanded use of cooperative aerial inspections; and the establishment of an international Center for the Prevention of Conflict, such as was recently done in Europe to review and assess the implementation of an expanding CSBMs regime. These are the kinds of subjects that should be discussed and considered in regional talks on Middle East arms control.

Moreover, there are precedents for this in the Middle Eastern context. Conventional wisdom seems to hold that arms control cannot and has not worked in the Middle East. This is mistaken, for there is far greater experience in the region with arms control than is often imagined. Soon after the signing of the November 11, 1973, cease-fire agreement between Israel and Egypt, the United States helped put into place a series of transparency measures, notwithstanding the fact that the two countries remained at war. These measures included inspections by United Nations forces, creation of limited-force zones, and air reconnaissance by U.S. aircraft. Further, since 1974, UN forces have managed on-site challenge inspections of Israeli and Syrian forces in the Golan Heights involving quantitative and geographic limitations on weapons deployments, even though both of these countries remain at war with one another and have had no direct talks to this day.[18] The Camp David accords between Israel and Egypt took transparency several steps further by providing for: air reconnaissance missions using sophisticated photography devices; manned and unmanned observation and detection posts equipped with various types of sensors and electronic detection devices; early-warning posts in designated areas; ground, naval, and air patrols; and on-site inspections, both routine and challenge, conducted by national teams. These activities are carried out by a third party, the United States, at the request of Israel and Egypt.[19]

These are but modest first steps toward arms control in the Middle East. There are numerous reasons why these efforts can be shown to be infeasible or unlikely to succeed. Ultimately, this may prove to be true given the history and problems of the Middle East. Nevertheless, such efforts should at least be tried—initially by the world's major arms-supplier nations and hopefully by the nations in the region as well. The dangers of not trying to take advantage of arms control possibilities in the post–Cold War, post–Gulf War world surely outweigh the risks involved in undertaking such an effort.

NOTES

1. "An Interim Report of the United States Institute of Peace's Study Group on Regional Arms Control Arrangements and Issues in the Post-War Middle East" (Washington, D.C.: United States Institute of Peace, 1991), p. 4. This

classic definition of arms control is drawn from Thomas Schelling and Morton Halperin, *Strategy and Arms Control*, rev. ed. (Washington, D.C.: Pergamon-Brassey, 1985), pp. 2–4.

2. "An Interim Report of the United States Institute of Peace's Study Group on Regional Arms Control Arrangements and Issues in the Post-War Middle East," p. 4.

3. Michael Nacht, Jay Winik, and Alan Platt, "The Middle East: What About Arms Control?" *Washington Post*, September 22, 1991, p. C3. For an excellent discussion of different paths to inadvertent conflict, see Alexander George, ed., *Avoiding War: Problems of Crisis Management* (Boulder: Westview Press, 1991), Part 7.

4. "After the Gulf War," *Foreign Affairs* 70, no. 4 (Fall 1991), p. 64.

5. Richard Grimmett, *Conventional Arms Transfers to the Third World, 1983–1990*, Congressional Research Service Report 91–578F, August 1991. For a detailed discussion of current trends among the major arms exporters to the Middle East, see Natalie Goldring, "The 'Big 5' Arms Suppliers and Their Major Recipients," Defense Budget Project, Washington, D.C., September 24, 1991.

6. William Hartung, "The Boom at the Arms Bazaar," *Bulletin of the Atomic Scientists* (October 1991), p. 15; "U.S. Arms Transfers: July 1991," *Arms Control Today* (September 1991), p. 37.

7. For a discussion of the growth of nonsuperpower arms exports to the Middle East during the 1980s, see Alan Platt, "European Arms Transfers and Other Suppliers [to the Middle East]," in Steven Spiegel, Mark Heller, and Jacob Goldberg, eds., *The Soviet-American Competition in the Middle East* (Lexington, Mass.: D.C. Heath, 1988), pp. 61–75.

8. Stockholm International Peace Research Institute, *SIPRI Yearbook 1990: World Armaments and Disarmament* (Oxford: Oxford University Press, 1990), Table 7.2, p. 228.

9. Andrew Ross, "The Arming of the Third World: Patterns and Trends," *SAIS Review* (Summer/Fall 1991).

10. For a more detailed discussion of the spread of ballistic missile technology in the Middle East and around the world, see Seth Carus, *Ballistic Missiles in the Third World: Threat and Response*, Washington Paper for the Center for Strategic and International Studies, Washington, D.C. (New York: Praeger, 1990); Janne Nolan, *Trappings of Power: Ballistic Missiles in the Third World* (Washington, D.C.: The Brookings Institution, 1991).

11. Charles Floweree and Brad Roberts, "Arms Control in the Middle East: Chemical Weapons," unpublished paper, January 1992, p. 2.

12. *The Washington Post*, June 11, 1990, p. 1.

13. Seth Carus, *Ballistic Missiles*, p. 29. This linkage was explicitly made by the United Nations Security Council in a 1987 study, S/18852, "Report of the Specialists Dispatched by the Secretary-General to Investigate Allegations of the Use of Chemical Weapons in the Conflict Between Iran and Iraq," May 8, 1987, p. 6. In the report it is stated that "if the [Geneva] Protocol [banning first use of chemical weapons] is irreparably weakened after 60 years of general international respect, this may lead, in the future, to the world facing the specter of the threat of biological weapons." This is requoted in Carus, "The Poor Man's Atomic Bomb?" p. 29n.

14. "Communique, Meeting of the Five on Arms Transfers and Non-Proliferation, Paris, 8th and 9th of July 1991," 1991.

15. For further discussion of sanctions, see Lewis Dunn and James Schear, "Combatting Chemical Weapons Proliferation: The Role of Sanctions and

Assurances," Occasional Paper 3 (Washington, D.C.: The Henry Stimson Center, 1991). Also, Jay Kosminsky, "Arsenal of Democracy: Defense Strategies for a Revolutionary Decade," *Policy Review* (Fall 1991), pp. 67–68.

16. One of the earliest efforts to delineate these two distinctive approaches to arms control in Europe is Richard Darilek, "The Future of Conventional Arms Control in Europe: A Tale of Two Cities: Stockholm, Vienna," *Survival* 24, no. 1 (January–February 1987), pp. 5–16.

17. "Transparency in the Middle East," *Arms Control Today* (May 1991), p. 8.

18. Michael Nacht, Jay Winik, and Alan Platt, "The Middle East: What About Arms Control?" p. C3. For a discussion of additional possible confidence- and security-building measures in the Middle East, see Thomas Hirschfeld, "Mutual Security Short of Arms Control," in Dore Gold, ed., *Arms Control in the Middle East* (Boulder: Westview Press, 1991), pp. 33–35.

19. Itshak Lederman, "The Arab-Israeli Experience in Verification and Its Relevance to Conventional Arms Control in Europe," Occasional Paper 2 (College Park, Md.: Center for International Security Studies, 1989).

13

Arms Control and the Resolution of the Arab-Israeli Conflict: An Arab Perspective

ABDEL MONEM SAID ALY

For more than four decades, the parties to the Arab-Israeli conflict have been involved in a deadly arms race. Arabs and Israelis have compiled massive amounts of conventional weapons. Over time, the two sides of the conflict have acquired the highest levels of technology in these weapons available in the world outside the major international powers. Furthermore, Israel has become a nuclear power. Most experts on the subject agree that Israel possesses not only nuclear capabilities but also nuclear warheads. In 1988 there were indications that Israel was involved in the development of thermonuclear warheads. Israel possesses both aircraft and missile delivery systems that are capable of reaching many Arab capitals. Finally, during the 1980s Israel introduced the space arms race into the Middle East.

The Israeli nuclear superiority helped ignite a new phase of the arms race in the Middle East. Failing to catch up with Israel in the nuclear field, Arab countries such as Syria, Iraq, and Libya started to build "above conventional" chemical mass destruction weapons. These countries, in addition to Egypt and Saudi Arabia, acquired or developed aircraft and missiles capable of reaching Israel.

The end result of the deadly arms race in the Middle East is an intolerable situation. Another Arab-Israeli war will mean massive devastation due to the very high level of destructive technologies. The Gulf War gives a glimpse of the level of destruction, if there is no resolution of the conflict and there is another Arab-Israeli war. Experience shows that the existing "no war—no peace" situation between Israel and the Arab states is only a prescription for disaster to the parties concerned and to world security. A concerted international effort is needed to deescalate the Arab-Israeli conflict and bring the parties to the negotiating table.

Fortunately, the Gulf War opened the door for intensive U.S. efforts to resolve the conflict. All the concerned parties have agreed to attend an international conference as framework for bilateral direct negotiations and to pave the way for cooperation in the fields of arms control, water, and the environment.

This chapter will attempt to contribute ideas for the negotiations on arms control. Some of these ideas are derived from the Arab-Israeli experience itself, others from European and world experience. The following discussion presents the point of view that peace and arms control arrangements can be mutually enhancing. A political settlement can guarantee a hospitable climate for deescalating the arms race, while arms control measures can create mutual confidence and stabilize a very destabilized situation.

ARMS CONTROL AND THE ARAB-ISRAELI CONFLICT

Throughout the Arab-Israeli conflict, Egypt, Syria, Jordan, and Israel have accepted arms control measures. The cease-fire and armistice agreements of 1948 and 1949 contained provisions for neutral and demilitarized zones on the Israeli borders with Egypt and Syria and in Jerusalem. The UN agreements that ended the Suez War in 1956 included provisions for UN peacekeeping forces on the two sides of the Egyptian-Israeli border. While Israel declined to accept this force on its side of the border, Egypt accepted and thus endorsed unilateral control over the movements of its forces in certain parts of Sinai. Moreover, between 1956 and 1967, Egypt unilaterally declined to deploy the main elements of its armed forces in Sinai as a clear signal that it had no intent of aggression against Israel.

While these measures were to deescalate existing conflicts, it was after the 1973 war that arms control measures were used to enhance the unfolding peace process. In the first disengagement agreement, in 1974, Egypt not only accepted limitations on its armed forces in certain areas east of the Suez Canal, but also accepted the existence of UN forces and curtailment of its air defenses west of the Suez Canal. In the second disengagement agreement, in 1975, Egypt accepted, in addition to demilitarized zones, certain confidence-building measures such as early-warning systems, electronic sensing, and notification of military movements to the UN force in Sinai.

The most ambitious of these arrangements came in 1979 in the Egyptian-Israeli peace treaty. Sinai was divided into three zones. Zone A would have no more than one mechanized infantry division, with up to 230 tanks and 22,000 troops. Zone B would have no more than four battalions of border units, equipped only with light weapons and up to 4,000 troops. Zone C would have only Egyptian civil police. On the Israeli side of the border, Zone D would have no more than four infantry battalions, with up to 4,000 personnel and 180 armored personnel vehicles, and military installations and field fortifications. These zones are supervised by early-warning systems and multinational forces.

The Egyptian-Israeli peace treaty extended the provisions of arms control to the territorial waters of Egypt and Israel. Article IV of the military Annex I to the treaty established a naval regime setting the following provisions:

1. Egypt and Israel may base and operate naval vessels along the coasts of Zone A and D, respectively.
2. Egyptian coast guard boats, lightly armed, may be stationed and operated in the territorial waters of Zone B to assist the border units in performing their functions in this zone.
3. Egyptian civil police equipped with light boats, lightly armed, shall perform normal police functions within the territorial waters of Zone C.
4. Nothing in this annex shall be considered as derogating from the right of the innocent passage of the naval vessels of either party.
5. Only civilian maritime ports and installations may be built in the zones.
6. Without prejudice to the provisions of this treaty, only those naval activities specially permitted by this annex shall be allowed in the zones and their territorial waters.

The provisions of the peace treaty have reduced dramatically the possibility of surprise attack for both Egypt and Israel. They have activated a process of military cooperation to monitor the implementation of the agreement in good faith. They have also established the precedent of asymmetrical balance of forces as one of the means to address Israeli insecurities in the exchange of territories. Finally, they have reduced to the minimum the possibility of accidental clashes whether on land, air, or sea.

For Egypt and the other Arab states, the Israeli nuclear capability is perceived not as a deterrent but a compellant. It is considered a destabilizing factor in the Middle East and a call for continuing the race in mass destructive weapons. Consequently, Egypt and Iran introduced a resolution in the twenty-ninth session of the UN, in 1974, for the establishment of a nuclear weapons–free zone (NWFZ) in the Middle East. This resolution has been reconfirmed in subsequent General Assembly meetings, and since 1980 there has been no opposition or abstention in votes on the resolution. Several Arab countries (Tunisia, Kuwait, Bahrain, Jordan, Mauritania, and Sudan) have participated in introducing these resolutions since 1975.

During the debates on the resolution, Egypt stressed four basic principles:

1. The states of the region should refrain from producing, acquiring, and possessing nuclear weapons.
2. The nuclear states should refrain from introducing nuclear weapons into the area or using nuclear weapons against states in the region.
3. An effective international safeguard system affecting both the nuclear weapons states and the states of the region should be established.
4. The establishment of an NWFZ in the Middle East should not prevent parties from enjoying the benefits of the peaceful uses of atomic energy, especially for economic development.

Furthermore, Egypt had gone as far as taking unilateral steps toward arms control. First, Egypt considered the Egyptian-Israeli peace treaty a way to curtail, if not eliminate, the Israeli nuclear arsenal. Although this did not materialize, Egypt ratified the Non-Proliferation Treaty (NPT) in 1982 and in 1986 froze all nuclear programs. Second, Egypt pursued through different international forums the ideal calling for establishing an NWFZ in the Middle East. Third, during the Paris Conference on Chemical Weapons in January 1989, Egypt supported the multilateral efforts to impose a total ban on chemical weapons (CWs) and asked that the chemical weapons convention include effective security guarantees for its members, not only against the use or the threat of use of CWs, but also against the use or the threat of use of any weapons of mass destruction. Countries that possess nuclear weapons refused this link. The Egyptian position was based on a plan proposed by President Mubarak that called for making the Middle East free of all weapons of mass destruction.

Earlier, in 1988, at the third UN General Assembly session on disarmament, Egypt introduced a new proposal regarding the establishment of an NWFZ in the Middle East. The proposal called, first, for all states of the region, as well as nuclear states beyond the region, to declare that they would not introduce nuclear weapons to the Middle East. Second, the secretary-general should be authorized to appoint a personal representative, or group of experts, to contact the states of the region with a view to formulating a model draft treaty to evolve specific measures for the creation of an NWFZ in the Middle East. Third, the International Atomic Energy Agency (IAEA) should be invited to prepare a study and submit recommendations for the necessary verification and inspection measures that would be implemented in conjunction with the establishment of the zone.

It should be mentioned that almost all the Arab states in the proposed zone are parties to the NPT (the exceptions are Algeria, Mauritania, Oman, and the United Arab Emirates). Those Arab countries that are parties to the NPT and have nuclear research reactors (Egypt, Iraq, and Libya) are all subject to safeguard agreements with the IAEA. Algeria, though not a party to the NPT, has placed its research reactor under IAEA safeguards. The three other Arab states not party to the NPT (Mauritania, Oman, and the United Arab Emirates) have no nuclear facilities that require international safeguarding.

ARMS CONTROL AND THE
RESOLUTION OF THE ARAB-ISRAELI CONFLICT

Since World War II, the Middle East has witnessed not only an increase in armed conflicts, but also a deadly arms race unparalleled in any other region of the world, except Europe. Although in this latter area a general reduction of tension and arms racing has taken place in the post–Cold War period, the situation in the Middle East has gone in the opposite direction. Although Israel continued to be the only nuclear power in the area, several Arab countries attempted to catch up in the nuclear field, notably Iraq. When they failed, these countries resorted to the acquisition of chemical and other mass destruction weapons. The problem has been compounded by the proliferation of advanced missiles and other advanced military technologies.

The last two Gulf crises have demonstrated that the Middle East problems are much larger than the Arab-Israeli conflict. However, this conflict remains a major one, certainly as far as arms control is concerned. Fortunately, the second Gulf crisis has created a general consensus in the United States, Europe, and the major powers that peace and security in the Middle East cannot prevail without limitations on the acquisition of arms, particularly mass destruction weapons. Security Council Resolution 687, for a permanent cease-fire in the Gulf, demands the elimination of all Iraqi chemical and biological weapons, the dismantling of nuclear facilities, and limitations on the range of ballistic missiles. What is important about this resolution is that it not only sets precedents in the Middle East context, but also states explicitly that these measures are taken as steps toward the goal of establishing a zone in the Middle East that is free of nuclear and other mass destruction weapons and their delivery systems (Article 14). Furthermore, the present U.S. efforts to settle the Arab-Israeli conflict, which were motivated by the Gulf crisis, are expected to include arms limitation talks, among many other issues.

The success of this attempt at peace will depend on the concerned parties to develop ideas that will enhance the prospects of peace and security in the Middle East. In October 1990, a group of experts presented to the UN secretary-general *A study on effective and verifiable measures which would facilitate the establishment of a Nuclear-Weapon-Free Zone in the Middle*

East (*UN DOC A/45/435 Document Studies Series*, 22). The study suggested practical measures to cap the Israeli nuclear capabilities by putting the Dimona reactor under the IAEA safeguards within the NPT system, which would keep the Israeli nuclear deterrent intact until further political steps are taken on the road leading Israel to accept the provisions of a nuclear weapons–free zone. The study introduces a host of other ideas applicable to the Middle East drawn from the European experience in arms control and confidence building. What is interesting about this study is that it does not confine itself to the nuclear field, but also proposes limitations on other mass destruction and conventional weapons, including missiles.

The study also merges several proposals for establishing an NWFZ in the Middle East, especially the Mediterranean. Going beyond the Mediterranean, the study states that "several sea areas may be considered for inclusion or 'thinning-out' [by inside or outside powers], measures in relation to the proposed zone in the Middle East. Both the Red Sea and the Persian Gulf may be enclosed or semi-enclosed within the zonal area. Prospective zonal areas have coasts in the Mediterranean, the Atlantic and the North-Western Indian Ocean. . . . The prospective zonal area would include a few international straits subject to the regime of transit passage, i.e., the straits of Gibraltar, Bab al Mandab, and Hormuz. Also important in this respect is the Suez Canal."[1]

What is lacking in this study, however, is a linkage between the establishment of the NWFZ in the Middle East and the overall settlement of conflicts, particularly the Arab-Israeli one. In this regard, it seems that a Conference on Security and Cooperation in the Middle East (CSCME) is required to be a proper forum to discuss and link military, economic, and political issues in the Middle East. This idea seems to be gaining acceptance in the United States, Europe, and the Middle East. Also lacking in this study is the time frame for introducing Israel to the NWFZ in the Middle East. Although certain asymmetries might be acceptable to facilitate agreements, symmetrical and reciprocal arrangements should be the norm at the end of the road. Therefore, if Israel keeps its nuclear weapons while safeguarding Dimona, these weapons should be phased out or reduced over a period of time as a confidence-building measure. Some of them could be eliminated as a result of international guarantees; others should be eliminated in a trade for peace treaties with Arab countries; the rest should be eliminated once full normalization of relations and different types of economic and functional cooperation are established. The same process should be applied to chemical weapons for both sides of the conflict. In this respect, arms control measures, along with other issues, should be part of the peace process, not separate from it.

In the peace process, destabilizing weapons should be curtailed. A ban on exporting cruise and long-range (more than 150 kilometers) ballistic and cruise missiles should be arranged among arms-exporting countries. The present Israeli plans to expand Israel's sea projection capabilities, particularly sea-launched, long-range conventional and nuclear missiles and advanced submarines, should be halted during the Arab-Israeli negotiations. This step would prevent triggering a new naval race that could make arms control measures difficult in the future. CBMs such as notification of naval movements and cooperative sea operations against drug smuggling or terrorist actions by regional powers could enhance both the possibilities of arms control and the mutual trust necessary for peace in the Middle East. Other CBMs, such as transparency measures, incidents-at-sea arrangements, notification of exercises, and prevention of dangerous military activities, could contribute to the achievement of this goal. It has to be understood, however, that the CBMs should not be a goal in themselves. They should be—as the case in Europe—an integral part of the political process to reduce tensions and deescalate conflicts in the Middle East. In fact, as presented above, the history of the Arab-Israeli conflict shows that demilitarized zones, curtailments of military movements, and CBMs have helped to deescalate conflicts and to achieve the first peace treaty between an Arab country and Israel.

NOTE

1. United Nations, *UN DOC A/45/435 Document Studies Series,* 22, p. 16 (New York: United Nations, 1991).

14

A Proposed Security Regime for an Arab-Israeli Settlement

M. Z. DIAB

The peace process that has been under way between Israel and the Arabs since October 1991 has generated a certain optimism that a settlement can be reached. This chapter will attempt to shed some light on the start of this process and the required security regime to uphold it if a settlement is achieved.

MUTUAL THREAT PERCEPTION

There is no doubt that the relationships of conflict among the parties in the Arab-Israeli dispute have generated one of the most hostile environments in the world. This situation is largely the result of a combination of factors that have molded and conditioned attitudes and perceptions on both sides. A brief review of these factors might help explain the crux of this relationship of mutual threat perception.

The Historical/Ideological Factor
Historically, the Arabs have regarded Israel as a bastion to protect Western imperialist interests in the Middle East. On one hand, for the Arabs, as they were struggling to liberate themselves from the yoke of colonialism in the 1940s and 1950s, the creation of Israel was nothing but an attempt to perpetuate the crumbling colonial system under another guise. On the other hand, the Jews looked upon Israel as the only solution to save them from the anti-Semitism inflicted upon them in Europe since the Diaspora, and that culminated in the Holocaust.

In the struggle against the colonial powers, the Eastern Arabs raised the banner of Arab nationalism as a rallying slogan. Consequently, the appearance of the Zionist movement, which aspired to establish a national home for the Jews in Palestine, was bound for a head-on collision with Arab nationalist aspirations.

The Political Factor

The birth of Israel in 1948 and the dispossession of the Palestinian people from their homeland ignited a conflict between Israel and its neighboring Arab countries in which each side viewed the other in terms of a zero-sum game. To the Arabs, Israel represented a real threat to their intrinsic, vital interests and national values. Israel was set up at the expense of Arab land and Arab people.

The present situation, where Israel occupies the West Bank, Gaza Strip, Golan Heights, and southern Lebanon, and where it continues to build settlements in the occupied territories and divert water resources to its sole advantage, only confirms the long-standing apprehension of the Arabs that Israel is an expansionist state. This perception is very significant, as Syria, Jordan, and Lebanon view this occupation of their territories with alarm, since it strikes at the heart of their vital security interests: land, water, and political stability. In addition, the continuation of this occupation means a denial of the right to self-determination and nationhood for the Palestinian people, which is a major cause of the political instability in Jordan and Lebanon.

Meanwhile, the Israelis have coupled their concept of security with the occupation of the aforementioned lands under various pretexts. In their eyes, Arab hostility toward the very idea of Israel is still simmering, although a peace treaty was signed with Egypt in 1979. Israel claims that its security and prosperity can be ensured only by adhering to this occupation and continuing to settle on these occupied territories to create faits accomplis. It may be justified in its fear for its security and national existence, but the surest way to guarantee this lies in meeting equitably the reasonable demands of the Arabs in order to allay *their* fears.

The Technological Factor

Israel is, for all intents and purposes, part and parcel of Western culture and technology, and the Arabs have viewed this symbiotic relationship with great apprehension. Seen as part of the underdeveloped world struggling for economic improvement, the Arabs have realized that they would always be at a disadvantage vis-à-vis Israel because of the gap in technological experience, which is relevant politically, economically, and militarily.

These three basic factors have actually become a vicious circle of mutual threat perception, so that every action, whether political or military, on the part of the antagonists contributes to the process that generates increased fear and suspicion in the whole arena. Is there a way to break this vicious circle? The answer is, guardedly, yes.

THE ROAD TO A PEACEFUL
SETTLEMENT AND ITS ELEMENTS

The crucial question now is where to proceed from the present situation. The answer depends in turn on responding to two important questions: Has the Arab position regarding the existence of Israel undergone any transformation? And is Israel willing to trade land for peace and be content with the borders of 1967?

The answer to the first question is strongly affirmative. The majority of the Arabs, particularly those who are directly concerned—Egypt, Syria, Jordan, Lebanon, and the Palestinians—have accepted Israel as a reality to coexist with. But for them the issue remains: What kind of Israel? However, one cannot answer the question regarding the Israeli position with any certainty because of the nature of Israeli society.

In my view, a turning point in the history of the Arab-Israeli conflict was the 1967 war. This war produced double-edged results. For the majority of Arabs, the 1967 defeat meant that Israel was de facto a reality they had to admit to and contend with. To some extent this reality was reinforced by Israel's nuclear capability, which was acquired to ensure its existence within the 1967 borders. In other words, the Arabs drew two important conclusions. First, the technological gap between Israel and the Arabs was so wide in every sphere that it made talk about the annihilation of Israel an absurd proposition. Second, in spite of Soviet support for the Arab side, the international community, particularly the superpowers, would not countenance the decisive defeat of Israel, let alone its disappearance. At the same time, the defeat and occupation of further Arab territory confirmed Arab fears, as previously mentioned, of an expansionist Israel that was developing at the expense of more Arab territory and water resources in the region. For the Israelis, the 1967 victory intoxicated them as they proved their prowess, but unfortunately it strengthened their greed and their disdain for the Arabs. Although the October 1973 war modified many perceptions and attitudes on both sides—indeed, it gave some Israelis a measure of sobriety—the problem remains essentially that Israel has caught itself up in a security dilemma of its own making. On the one hand, due to international and regional factors, Israel cannot impose a strategic surrender on the Arabs through breaking their will and forcing them to accept the status quo. And further, Israel lacks adequate military resources for this objective. On the other hand, the coupling of its security with the occupation and denial to Palestinians of their national rights will only lead to the continuation of the conflict.

However, one crucial result of the 1967 war, which has transformed immeasurably the nature of the conflict, is that it is no longer a zero-sum game, but has become a non-zero-sum one. This development is very important, for it has changed the nature of the conflict from "pure conflict" into one "where conflict is mixed with mutual dependence." Hence, such transformation would enable a trade-off in peace for land and "mutual accommodation."[1]

Although Egypt and Syria pursued efforts sponsored mainly by the United States to reach a settlement following the October war of 1973—with Syria accepting Resolutions 338 and 242—these efforts collapsed in October 1977. At the time, Israel refused to go to an international conference under the joint sponsorship of the United States and Soviet Union at which the PLO would be present. This consequently led the Egyptian president, Anwar Sadat, to conclude a separate peace treaty with Israel in 1979. The treaty was opposed by the majority of Arab states, particularly Syria and the Palestinians, since it would not help to respond to the demands of the Arabs that Israel withdraw fully from the occupied territories of 1967 and that the Palestinians be allowed to exercise their right to self-determination.

For Syria, the separate peace meant a devastating blow to its strategy to contain Israel, which called for reaching a comprehensive settlement based on balanced regional power relationships. When President Hafez Assad assumed power in 1970, he maintained that a peaceful settlement with Israel required "Arab solidarity" as a counterpoise and deterrent to Israeli expansionist policies and that only a comprehensive settlement on all fronts could lead eventually to peaceful coexistence. For him, such balanced regional power relationships were complemented by the central strategic balance between the two superpowers.

However, two basic factors have helped lend new impetus to current U.S. efforts to work for a settlement between Israel and Syria, Lebanon, Jordan, and the Palestinians. The first factor was the end of the Cold War and the advent of the new détente between the superpowers. When this process started in the mid-1980s, the Arabs (especially Syria) realized that they could no longer rely on the Soviet Union to form a counterbalance to the U.S. backing of Israel. For Syria, the end of the Cold War has also meant that its objective of building strategic parity with Israel, namely to have the offensive capability to recover the Golan Heights through its own efforts alone, cannot be fully realized.

The second factor was the 1991 Gulf War, following the Iraqi invasion of Kuwait in 1990. This war produced two paradoxical results. On the one hand, the Arab side in the Arab-Israeli equation has been weakened further, owing to the political disarray among fellow Arabs and the curtailing of Iraq's military capabilities, which it brought upon itself by waging the war. On the other hand, the coalition between Egypt, Syria, and Saudi Arabia has been further cemented to such a degree that it has made it possible for Syria to join the new U.S.-Arab relationship. This nexus has resulted from the coincidence between Arab common interests per se and Western interests to protect the status quo in the Gulf.

Hence, the U.S. initiative to convene a peace conference in Madrid in October 1991, on the basis of Resolutions 242 and 338, was welcomed by Syria, Jordan, Lebanon, Egypt, and the Palestinians. Although from the Syrian point of view the optimum conditions for achieving a settlement that satisfies Arab demands do not fully exist, the fact that the United States is seeking stability in the Middle East by balancing its interests between Israel and the Arabs to reach a settlement was seen by the Syrian leadership as a compensational political factor for the demise of the Soviet counterweight and the end of the Cold War.[2]

With regard to the essential elements of a settlement, the overall majority of the Arab states and the international community agree that any settlement has to be based on Resolution 242, passed in 1967, and Resolution 338, passed in 1973; therefore, the bottom line for the Arab position in this situation, as I see it, is as follows:

First, Israel has to commit itself to withdraw from the West Bank, Gaza Strip, Golan Heights, and southern Lebanon (in accordance with Resolution 425 [1978], which was passed following the invasion of Lebanon). Second, there has to be a special status for East Jerusalem, perhaps neutralization, so that symbolic Arab control can be restored. Third, the Palestinian people should be allowed to exercise their full legitimate rights to self-determination and to establish their own state, whether in confederation or federation with Jordan.

An Israeli agreement to these broad terms of a settlement would transform the conflict from violent into peaceful means and would thereby enter the phase of conflict control as a step toward full peaceful relations and ultimate resolution of the conflict.[3] Such a settlement would surely alleviate a great deal of Arab apprehension of an expansionist Israel and in turn assure the Israelis that the residue of Arab hostility would gradually be eradicated, thus granting them a true and real sense of security. Determining how this settlement could be reached and the time scale involved to implement it is the task of the current negotiations under the umbrella of the peace conference initiated by the United States with the cooperation of the former Soviet Union.

Although the Palestinians want an early settlement with Israel to save their land, it seems that the Syrians favor a more gradual program toward a peaceful settlement, judging by their pronouncements regarding their overall objectives. In joining the peace process, Syrian objectives are short-, medium-, and long-term, as well as minimal and maximal. The time frame and the extent of goals intersect, but do not necessarily coincide.

Short-Term Objectives

It is possible to detect five short-term objectives. First, the immediate Syrian aim is to build on the new U.S.-Arab relationship by strengthening the hand of the present U.S. administration vis-à-vis the U.S. Congress, which is the basic power base of Israel. Second, to make sure that President Bush is reelected, by giving him a foreign policy success. He has publicly undertaken to work for a settlement, which places him under a moral and political obligation unknown by previous U.S. presidents. The fact that under his leadership the United States is trying for the first time to balance its interests between Israel and the Arabs and seek stability in the region—thanks to the Gulf War— is encouraging. Third, to tie down a right-wing Israeli government to the peace process it was forced to join by U.S. pressure. Fourth, to increase the contradictions in the domestic Israeli arena in order to help in forming a government more amenable to accepting a settlement following an election, whether Shamir stays on or not. Fifth, to maximize the pressure on Israel to halt building settlements in the occupied territories.

Medium-Term Objectives

One can think of two basic medium-term aims that are sought by Syria. First, to attempt to strengthen Arab political and military power, hoping that the present Iraqi regime will disappear, making it easy to rebuild Arab consensus and solidarity. This would put the Arab side in a better bargaining position. Second, once President Bush assumes his second term, he would be in a much stronger position to put pressure on Israel to accept the principle of withdrawal and allow the Palestinians to exercise their political rights.

Long-Term Objectives

If the course of events that Syria envisages unfolds over the next three to five years, it is possible to contemplate the conclusion of a comprehensive settlement on all fronts comprising two basic elements. First, the Palestinians would be in a position to exercise their right to self-determination. Second, the implementation of full Israeli withdrawal from the West Bank, Gaza Strip, East Jerusalem, Golan Heights, and southern Lebanon.

The Syrian attitude is that a full-fledged peace treaty with Israel is impossible without a total settlement; the peace must be a comprehensive one. Israel would be deluding itself if it mistakenly thought that it could drive a wedge between the Arab partners, especially between Syria and the Palestinians. The commitment of Syria to the Palestinian cause is not only ideological, an article of faith for any incumbent regime, but also a matter of vital national security, as the refugee status of the Palestinians in Lebanon, Syria, and Jordan and their being denied their national rights are causes of political instability in all three countries. This is contrary to what some Western observers, blindly following the Israeli line, maintain—that those three states exploit the Palestinian problem for their own parochial domestic interests.

If there is an agreement on the basic principles of a settlement as outlined above, obviously there has to be a security regime in place to underpin it and to guarantee stability in the region. This regime could be divided into two types of mutually reinforcing measures: (1) establishing confidence- and security-building measures; and (2) establishing an arms control regime to regulate the military balances among the main antagonists.

CONFIDENCE- AND SECURITY-BUILDING MEASURES (CSBMS)

It would be a mistake to attempt to transplant the European model of CSBMs directly to the Arab-Israeli conflict environment, for several reasons. One major problem is the interrelationship of regional disputes in the three main areas of actual or potential conflict: between the Arabs and Israel; among the Gulf states; and inter-Arab disputes. It could be argued, however, that it is possible to identify the core of the confrontation states in the Arab-Israeli conflict: Egypt, Syria, Jordan, Lebanon, and Israel. Yet, the fact that the Arab states are inextricably part of the Arab system and Gulf subsystem makes it hard to use any unified criteria of CSBMs for all states involved without affecting their security requirements in relation to other conflicts or potential ones.

Second, the confrontation in Europe between Eastern and Western blocs did not involve disputed territories and a dispossessed people demanding its legitimate right to nationhood, such as with the Palestinians. What prompted the Europeans and the United States to adopt CSBMs in the Helsinki and Stockholm agreements was basically the spiraling of the technological arms race and the redundancy of the role of the threat and use of force in conducting interstate relations. In the Arab-Israeli conflict, the impact of technology is less important and ranks very much second to the political issues at stake. Moreover, the belligerent states still regard the threat and use of force as a legitimate means to protect their vital interests. Both sides of the divide regard such a principle as a useful tool to deter and/or compel their opponents either in actual armed hostilities or in negotiations.

Third, because the key concept of CSBMs is transparency and openness, in a tense environment like the Middle East they may further exacerbate the existing mutual suspicion, as each side fears revealing and exposing military vulnerabilities.

Nevertheless, the situation should not be so discouraging as to preclude any new thinking on suitable CSBMs. I would contend that if Israel, seen as the stronger side of the conflict equation, were to take the bold step of committing itself to meet essential Arab prerequisites to a settlement, the door would be open to establish CSBMs appropriate to the particular characteristics of the conflict. Such a decision by Israel would greatly help isolate the Arab-Israeli conflict from others in the region. Thus, it would be more fruitful to envisage CSBMs as complementary to, or simultaneous with, implementing a comprehensive settlement.

The following steps might be taken to minimize tension in the interim period, while the unfolding phases of the settlement are implemented:

1. Put an end to the state of belligerency in return for freezing further development of Israeli settlements in the occupied territories.

2. Create buffer zones on both sides of the international borders as the Israelis withdraw from the West Bank, Gaza Strip, Golan Heights, and Lebanon.

3. Impose restrictions on the deployment of the number of troops and the type of weapons systems deployed in the areas adjacent to the buffer zones.

4. Set up monitoring and observation posts in the buffer zones on both sides of the borders to be jointly manned by UN observers, the parties concerned, and personnel from the five permanent members of the UN Security Council.

5. Establish a crisis management center,[4] possibly in Jerusalem, under UN auspices, to deal with dangerous border incidents that may escalate. The center could also be useful as a channel of communication to intercept hostilities that might be precipitated by miscalculation or misunderstanding arising from actions of a member state within the security regime that may not be related to the bilateral relationship per se—for example, if Syria were to deploy troops along the Turkish or Iraqi borders. The center should be headed by a high-ranking UN diplomat who would have direct access to foreign and defense ministers and even heads of governments or states. Obviously, the center would be more effective if it is also staffed by representatives of the members of the security regime in order to coordinate with the observation posts and the governments concerned.

6. Work out provisions to enable surveillance whether by satellite or aerial reconnaissance to guard against the threat of surprise attack. Such a measure, however, could deal only with the element of military capability. With regard to the thorny problem of interpretation of intentions, the crisis management center would contribute considerably.

7. Have all participants in the regime agree to notify the crisis management center of major military movements, maneuvers, and mobilization that might be relevant to internal or external developments. All participants in the regime must agree to do this.

8. Ensure that all parties to the agreement renounce unilaterally and, even better, multilaterally the first use of force and abstain from attacking civilian targets.

The adoption of these measures, along with a timetable for putting into effect an agreed settlement, would undoubtedly create an atmosphere of improved confidence and trust that would, in turn, help greatly to decrease the mutual threat perception problem.

ARMS CONTROL MEASURES

It would be foolish to believe that a settlement between the antagonists in the Arab-Israeli conflict should automatically entail complete disarmament. Decades of mutual suspicion and armed hostility have made each side wary and prone to think of worst-case scenarios. What one can hope for realistically in the short term is to establish a security regime that responds to the essential security requirements of every party involved. The regime's basic objective would be to bolster the envisaged settlement and thereby diminish the mutual fear and apprehension of its members.

The cornerstone of the security regime would be a mutually stable deterrent. It may well be argued that conventional deterrence is inherently unstable because of the difficulty in accurately estimating both tangible and intangible components of military strength. Nonetheless, one should not be daunted from attempting to realize the best available option. Leaving the arms race unbridled would only result in increasing tension and thereby become a self-fulfilling prophecy, in that each side is bent on destroying the other.

Any arms control system considered has to be addressed on two levels: regional and external.

Regional Level

On the regional level, the starting point would be for the parties of the regime to examine the security requirements of each participant to determine the possible threats to which each might be exposed. The proposed multilateral talks in the U.S. peace initiative suggest arms control as one of the topics to be covered. However, such discussions would most probably concentrate on arms supplies and weapons of mass destruction, whereas defining the military relationships among the members of the regime would be reached bilaterally.

The second major task would be to search for the appropriate military posture that would meet these requirements and also be sufficient to respond to any assumed threats. One may contend that it is easy to theorize about such a scheme, but patience, hard work, and goodwill to implement a political settlement offer the best chance to rein in the current arms race.

With regard to practical steps that must be taken in drawing up the security regime, I would suggest confronting the following issues:

1. Each party should define and clarify its strategic concept and its consequent military doctrine. As mentioned above, this doctrine should be of an essentially defensive nature.

2. All parties must gradually adopt force structures that are in line with the agreed-to military doctrines. The preliminary stages of restructuring military forces do not automatically mean the reduction, let alone the elimination, of certain types of weapon systems. For instance, air defense systems should be encouraged and made more sophisticated. But later on, any reduction in weapons must be based on the asymmetries in force structures.

Emphasis should be placed on the reduction and eventual elimination of the most destabilizing systems, such as long-range missiles and chemical and biological weapons (CBWs). Again, all sides should be encouraged to take advantage of precision guided munitions (PGM) defensive systems in order to strengthen conventional deterrence. Even though some military analysts are still dubious about the military impact of PGMs, recent wars have proved their effectiveness in minimizing casualties, particularly among civilians. They also have the advantage of enabling a reduction in the number of aircraft and tanks as the mainstays of battle.

3. The most difficult issue continues to be the Israeli nuclear capability. In the initial stages, Israel, being the only country in the region that has such a capability following the dismantling of the Iraqi attempt, has to sign the Nuclear Non-Proliferation Treaty and submit its nuclear facilities to international inspection. If in the short term Israel feels more secure in retaining some of its military nuclear capability to enable it to withdraw to its pre-1967 borders, this could be considered, on condition that this remaining capability must be eliminated once the final stage of the settlement is achieved. A regional nuclear weapons–free zone could then be declared. In this instance, it is worth noting that it is doubtful whether the Arab states would abandon their chemical weapons capabilities unless Israel makes such a commitment.

4. The parties of the security regime would have to undertake not to involve themselves in military alliances that impinge on the Arab-Israeli security environment and that may lead to changes in the military balances agreed to. In this way, the Israeli argument, that it has to take into consideration the military capabilities of the Arab Gulf states, Iraq, and Libya in conjunction with the members of the regime, would lose its validity. The Arab states are part of an Arab system, and they are duty bound to participate in its dynamics. Hence, a commitment by Egypt or Syria, for example, to strengthen the security of the Arab Gulf states should not cause alarm to Israel, since such a pledge is directed to different security needs. What is essential is that the parties to the regime should not permit the stationing of foreign armies not required for domestic reasons, for example, the case of the Syrian presence in Lebanon.

Admittedly, the outer ring or Gulf states' interaction with the inner ring states—Egypt, Syria, Jordan, and Lebanon—may create concern for Israel. It is possible to envisage a solution on two levels. First, on the regional level, the Arab states that have no common borders with Israel should be encouraged and even pressured to sign a peace treaty, or at least a nonaggression pact with Israel once a settlement has been reached. Second, the external arms suppliers have to maintain a balance between the defensive requirements of those latter Arab states and the need not to undermine the Arab-Israeli military balances that may arise from the proposed regime.

5. The theaters of disengagement should be divided into two main areas (since the Egyptian-Israeli peace treaty is still valid). The Jordanian-Palestinian theater should be treated as one entity. Therefore, the idea that a future Palestinian state has to be disarmed entirely is unrealistic and would be of advantage only to Israel. What could be accepted by the Arab side is to establish the Palestinian state as a kind of buffer zone and place restrictions on some types of its weapon systems, particularly in number.

The same reasoning could be applied to the Syrian-Lebanese theater, since Syria is vulnerable to an outflanking Israeli movement through the Beka'a Valley. The Israeli argument that the Syrian-Lebanese treaty of May 1991 poses a threat to its security is rather shallow. The treaty was a measure to stabilize Lebanon when the civil war ended;[5] following the strengthening of the Lebanese army and Israeli withdrawal from southern Lebanon, there will be no need for Syrian military presence.

6. An effective regime of on-site inspection and verification has to be devised to police the security regime. The best candidate for this task is the UN, which should be backed up by observers from the five permanent members of the UN Security Council.

As for policing the buffer zones, UN forces are already in Lebanon and Syria, so it is possible to augment and strengthen them with contingents from the five permanent members of the UN Security Council. These contingents would have to be stationed on both sides of the international borders so that they could act as trip-wire units that would alert and activate the Security Council should hostilities break out. The presence of these units should also be extended to the Jordanian-Palestinian theater.

In this context, the Egyptian-Israeli regime of disengagement and the experience gained from policing the subsequent demilitarized zones, in addition to the Israeli-Syrian disengagement agreement of 1974, offer some lessons to draw on. However, one must bear in mind differences in topography and the type of threats that may occur.

7. The UN Security Council should guarantee the implementation of the political settlement and its accompanying security regime. This international guarantee should include provisions that oblige the

guarantors, either unilaterally or collectively, to supervise effectively the implementation, and thereby include appropriate penalties in case a party should decide to renounce its commitments partly or totally.

External Level

In May 1991, President Bush put forward a proposal addressed to major arms suppliers to try to control the regional arms race by imposing restrictions on the supply of conventional and unconventional weapons. The initiative was met with mixed response among the antagonists of the Arab-Israeli conflict. The reason for this is that weapons are the symptoms and not basically the cause of conflicts. It is true that certain kinds of weapons may have a destabilizing influence and increase tension and the likelihood of war by miscalculation, but in most cases one should not put the cart before the horse. It must be noted, however, that quite clearly no regional arms control regime could ever be effective without the agreement of the major arms suppliers to the parties of the regime to act within its limitations.

The U.S. initiative has two basic parts. The first one deals with conventional arms, and the second deals with missiles and nuclear, biological, and chemical weapons. With regard to the first part, it would be futile and premature to ask the antagonists to forswear the acquisition of conventional weapons before reaching an agreed settlement. International arms suppliers are now so numerous that the task of enforcing an agreement is not an easy one, owing to the political and financial motives that exist. Consequently, an agreement among the external suppliers has to be linked to the political settlement and the security regime envisaged for the Arab-Israeli conflict. Then, and only then, arms purchases made by the parties involved in the regime could be judged in light of their defensive needs, such as identifying the need to phase out obsolete weapons systems. Another defect in the U.S. initiative is that it does not take into account the highly developed, indigenous Israeli military industry, which puts the Arab side at a disadvantage.

As for the second part of the U.S. initiative put forward by President Bush, it is realistic and should be welcomed, provided that it is adhered to by all states concerned, both regional and external. However, the initiative must be made more powerful and resolute by demanding the creation of a nuclear weapons–free zone rather than merely declaring "support" for such an endeavor. What is actually required is a solemn undertaking and binding agreement by Israel to relinquish its nuclear military capability once a political settlement has been reached and implemented and a security regime set up. The signing of such an agreement should be left until the last hour to avoid being prey to the vagaries of the Israeli outlook on security, depending on the government in power. The advantage of binding Israel by agreement from the start is that it would make it easier for Arab states to disarm themselves gradually of their chemical weapons. Rightly or wrongly, the Arabs regard chemical weapons as their only available insurance against Israeli nuclear blackmail if Israel were to attempt to impose a strategic surrender upon them.

CONCLUSION

In the final analysis, the prospects for controlling the Arab-Israeli conflict by reaching a settlement are now much better than at any time in its history. It would be a tragic error on the part of Israel to miss this opportunity to move away from conflict and toward cooperation. If some Israelis still believe that nuclear weapons and occupation will compel and subdue the Arab will and force them to unconditional surrender, then in the light of what has been considered in this chapter, they are very much mistaken. Indeed, the option of resorting to limited-liability wars will always be available as long as power relationships are subject to change. However, the Arabs have come full circle to accept the reality of Israel and its essential security needs, though they strongly believe that their vital interests and national values are at stake if their just demands are not met. Israel ought not to lose sight of one fundamental generalization in history, namely, that there can be no stable status quo as long as there are states that are dissatisfied and determined to change a disadvantageous status quo as they perceive it.

The current peace process initiated by President George Bush may offer a window of opportunity through which the Arabs and Israelis can learn to coexist peacefully. The question now remains as to whether Israel can face up to the challenge of peace.

NOTES

1. See Thomas C. Schelling, *The Strategy of Conflict* (London: Oxford University Press, 1960), p. 83.

2. There are two interpretations concerning the end of the Cold War: some Arabs regard it as a blessing because Israel has lost its value as a protector of Western interests in the Middle East; others see the event as a destabilizing factor of the international balance—which has allowed U.S. dominance—to the disadvantage of the Arabs.

3. According to the moderate ideological view of Arab nationalists, peaceful coexistence with Zionism cannot be attained until Israel is fully absorbed in the Arab system. In other words, although Israel would maintain its Jewish character, it should eventually accept a binational state with the Arab Palestinians in order to *resolve* the conflict in the strict sense. Of course, conflict control implies the end of belligerency and probably the signing of peace treaties after Israel completely withdraws and grants the Palestinians their self-determination, but it does not mean the *resolution* of conflict, which comes later on in the process.

4. The idea of a crisis management center was originally suggested by Professor Yair Evron of Tel Aviv University, although in a different form.

5. Officially the Ta'if Agreement of 1989 put an end to the civil war in Lebanon.

15

Arms Control in the Middle East: A European Perspective

Harald Müller

The term "Europe" is used in this chapter to mean those European states that are members of the European Community (EC). Of course, Europe is larger than the Twelve. But the EC is the magnetic core around which the integration of the old continent will progress—or fail. And, with all its shortcomings, it is today the only organization in Europe that approaches the quality of an "actor" in matters of conduct in international affairs.

Europe's interest in a peaceful Middle East is fairly obvious. The continent is undergoing a delicate period of rapid change in which there is little use for lingering instability and violence nearby. The Europeans receive half to two-thirds of their petroleum imports from the Middle East, and that percentage is rising. And at least the southern rim of the EC is already gravely concerned about hypothetical threats arising from the spread in the Middle East and North Africa of weapons of mass destruction and their intermediate-to-long-range delivery systems. No responsible defense official in Rome has forgotten the Scud missile fired at the island of Lampedusa as revenge for the U.S. air raid on Tripoli in 1986.

The following chapter discusses, first, specific Western European experiences that could be applied to arms control elsewhere. Second, some general conclusions from the East-West and particularly European arms control process that should be taken into account when regional arms control starts in the Middle East. Third, scope for action for the Europeans in this process.

SPECIFIC WESTERN EUROPEAN
ARMS CONTROL EXPERIENCES

The main asset EC-Europe brings into arms control negotiations is the most extensive experience with regional arms control anywhere in the world. Not all of these experiences were organized by and confined to EC countries, of course. But what is unique is the density of arms control networks by which these countries (and particularly the old Federal Republic of Germany) were covered. The following discussion does not address the more obvious gains made in the last five years—confidence-building measures under the Stockholm agreement, the INF (Intermediate Nuclear Forces) treaty, and the CFE treaty—but rather agreements and practices that have become so routine that they have hardly been noticed in recent years.

NATO Force Planning

Starting with a less than obvious example, NATO's force planning process can rightly be viewed from an arms control perspective. While its purpose was quite different—to softly force member states to do what NATO's military authorities thought necessary to balance the Warsaw Treaty Organization's power—what the process effectively did was to give information, year by year, on force structure and procurement planning. On the basis of this high transparency, member states knew what to expect for the foreseeable future in terms of the troop strength and armament of their closest neighbors (in reality, states always promised more than they implemented). Granted, this was done within an alliance. But among the countries opening up the arcane activities of their defense establishments were countries that had fought bitter wars against each other. For a peacetime alliance, the practice was revolutionary, and the principle of open force planning is a pivot for regional confidence building.

The West European Union Agency
for the Control of Armaments

Second, widely overlooked by analyses of arms control, the Agency for the Control of Armaments of the West European Union (WEU) has collected, over more than thirty years, an extensive experience in controlling conventional arms (and chemical weapons nonproduction). The main political aim of the agency was, of course, to make sure that West Germany did not trespass the limits imposed by the conditions under which it was admitted to the Brussels treaty. WEU inspectors did what CFE inspectors are now starting to do: visit equipment storage sites, count items, look at units and their configured equipment sets, and so on.

The agency has also produced a couple of highly interesting proposals for conventional arms control schemes that were largely put aside for CFE, partly because NATO did not want the WEU to steal the show on arms control in Europe and partly because some of the proposals appeared too complex to realize. Yet, the notion of tagging equipment with tamper-proof tags is very attractive in areas such as the Middle East, where the influx of weaponry is difficult to channel and where the distrust in governmental structures with low transparency might make more intrusive and detailed methods of verification advisable if not indispensable.

EURATOM

In the nuclear field, EURATOM, the oldest multinational inspectorate for nuclear installations, offers lessons for a region that—if it tackles the difficult problem of setting up a regional structure for confidence building in the nuclear sector—is likely to need far more exacting requirements than even a strengthened International Atomic Energy Agency safeguards system could provide.

EURATOM is remarkable in four different aspects. First, its inspectorate is multinational, drawn from the member states; such an arrangement would give Middle East member states a chance to inspect one another. But the Middle East would need to go a step further and include a clause stating that an Israeli inspector would automatically be part of the inspection team in each Arab state, and a Syrian or Egyptian inspector would participate in each visit to Israel; no such clause existed in the EURATOM treaty, but it is understood that informally, in the formation years, such special interests were recognized. Second, EURATOM has unlimited rights of access to designated and suspected facilities and is authorized to deal directly with the operators, not with state authorities. Third, EURATOM has the right to apply sanctions and fines directly to operators who fail to cooperate or who breach their obligations. And fourth, the Community formally owns all fissile material on the territory of the member states and has the hypothetical authority to remove material from a member country if needed—though this authority has never been exercised, the principle might well be considered for the Middle East.

EURATOM offers another interesting experience that may be applicable elsewhere (and will, in fact, be applied in the new regional verification scheme between Argentina and Brazil): the integration and collaboration among the state, the regional verification organization, and the global verification body—the IAEA. Although competition and rivalry has at times prevented this collaboration from working smoothly, the principle is important: the overlay of different organizations that complement each other and give confidence to the region as well as to the worldwide community of states.

Fourth, EURATOM is interesting because it combines the utilization of nuclear energy for peaceful purposes with the verification and confidence-building function in a regional context. Several countries in the Middle East are interested in harnessing nuclear energy. Egypt, Israel, and Syria are all looking for new sources of electricity because they lack sufficient domestic energy resources. For the Middle East, the idea originally embodied in the Rome treaties but never realized because of the commercial preferences of the member governments for domestic "champion" companies, would make tremendous sense: the joint management of the nuclear energy sector by one umbrella company with an international staff and serving an interconnected power grid. Such an institution would not obviate the need for strict verification, as it would not deal with the possibility of clandestine facilities. Yet, it would provide each of the parties a far better insight into the nuclear establishments of its partners and serve as an additional asset for creating warning signs if one of them should embark on a more sinister adventure.

Transferring Experience:
European–Middle East Seminars

How can experiences be transferred, and to what ends? It would be conceivable to hold a series of seminars during which Arab and Israeli governmental, military, and nuclear officials will be briefed over the legal structures, institutional settings, technical requirements, and procedural practices of time-honored arms control schemes. Participants may be invited to participate in a joint IAEA-EURATOM inspection at a power plant to check whether model tags developed by the WEU are tamper-proof, and so on. The purpose is to familiarize key staff that ideas that must look rather bold and theoretical in a region like the Middle East now are not only feasible but they work. Such seminars and visits would also give both sides the opportunity to look at options in a context free from the stress and inevitable competitive efforts of an international organization. They offer the psychological advantage that Middle East participants from all camps will be in the same position—trying to learn "how the Europeans did it" and, maybe, defending themselves collectively against the real or supposed arrogance of the "teachers"!

GENERAL EXPERIENCES FROM THE
EUROPEAN ARMS CONTROL PROCESS

Apart from the four detailed propositions presented in the preceding sections, there are five more general lessons from the European experience with arms control that should be considered, from the beginning, in any Middle East arms control process.

The External Environment of Arms Control

First, intra-European (that is, among the Western European countries) confidence building, arms control, and integration worked under two highly important external conditions: (1) the strong support, encouragement, and, at times, arms-twisting by the United States, the dominant external power; and (2) the presence of what was seen at the time as an overwhelming Soviet threat against which the Western Europeans had to play down their own conflicts and grievances. This second condition, of course, does not apply in the

Middle East, where the states engaged in arms control are threats against each other. All the more important is the first factor: a consistent, balanced, and strong involvement of those external powers whose influence might create favorable conditions for the whole protracted process of arms control. These powers include the United States, the former Soviet Union, and the European Community. The European role would be to steer a middle course between the two superpowers, whose traditional biases, pro-Israel for the United States and pro-Arab for the Soviets, are well known.

The Need for Mutual Recognition

Second, arms control cannot work as long as the parties neither recognize nor speak with each other. The long-standing West German policy of denying the legitimacy of the East German regime may have been rooted in perfectly honorable issues, as we saw after the breakdown of the Honecker government; yet, it was utterly counterproductive for the goal of reducing tensions and armaments levels in Europe. Even an enemy of highly doubtful character must be recognized as a partner to speak to if any agreements are to be reached. This is of particular importance when, as in the Middle East, nonrecognized parties are armed and must be counted as a factor—of whatever weight—in a regulated configuration of troop strength and arms limitation. This means breaking several taboos in the Middle East, not the least of which is the refusal of Israel to talk with the PLO and the recalcitrance of some Arab states to deal with Israel directly.

The Connection to Political Dispute Settlement

Third, arms control is unlikely to work unless basic territorial issues have been resolved. Even SALT I was achieved only after (through German treaties with Poland, Czechoslovakia, and the Soviet Union; the Basic Agreement between the two German states; and the four-powers agreement regulating access to Berlin) the specter of German revanchism and a Soviet assault on West Berlin had been defused. And the modest confidence-building measures in the Helsinki Act were agreed on only in the context of the ten principles, declaring the status quo in Europe changeable only by peaceful means. Confidence can be built only when there is no deep mistrust that one's existence is threatened by the intentions of one's neighbor; and arms will not be reduced unless territorial disputes that induce states to make and procure arms in the first place are reduced to a manageable level of virulence. This does not necessarily mean that territorial settlement must precede serious arms control. But it suggests that both must proceed in parallel and that we should not burden arms control with too much hope unless we have at least designed a procedure to solve more fundamental political issues.

Transparency and Democratization

In addition, the leeway for achieving breakthroughs for arms control remains strictly limited if the political systems of one or more participants do not allow for far-reaching transparency, openness, and internal control. Arms control negotiations and agreements were not useless in the European theater (more about this in the next paragraph). They helped to achieve marginally better understanding and were thus worthwhile. But they did not become, as hoped, a self-sustaining pillar of regional security until the Soviet Union adopted glasnost, a policy that permitted far more insights into its military policy; far-reaching, intrusive verification measures; and, as an organic synergism between greater internal openness, pluralism, and control on the one hand and international inspection on the other hand, a qualitatively new degree of mutual trust. Only the internal change—democratization and a visible movement toward a market economy even before the August 1991 revolution—helped to create the INF and CFE treaties, which contributed greatly to stabilizing the military balance and the building-down of a highly militarized conflict. Turning to the Middle East again, this analysis makes it advisable to tone down the unrealistic expectations regarding the contributions arms control can make. The Middle East contains too many countries with arcane decisionmaking, and even in Israel the fog of secrecy covers much of the country's armaments and military policy—not the least in the nuclear sector. Thus, arms control must be accompanied by a process of not only dispute settlement, but also internal democratization.

Arms Control as a Learning Process

Despite these warnings, it makes sense to enter arms control negotiations, because the European negotiations process—and the U.S.-Soviet history of arms control negotiations—bears out another important lesson: the importance of training, education, and the development of specialized expertise, as well as the interaction, over months and even years, of medium- to high-level staff members in the military services, defense departments, and foreign offices. Literally generations of diplomats learn how the other side is thinking about its security. Problems are understood and solutions examined in joint thought experiments. Worst enemy images are unlearned: many arms control experts in the Soviet Union supported perestroika and glasnost and ended up in the camp supporting unilateral arms control. On the U.S. side, the support lent by former negotiators on the ABM treaty was impressive. Arms control is the best training available for learning the ways of common security. Even if it does not result immediately in far-reaching agreements, it is still worthwhile for this long-term effect.

WHAT THE EUROPEANS CAN DO

The European scope for action falls into three categories: do not make things worse; offer impartial services to foster negotiations and agreements; and work with other outside powers to apply leverage to cooperative parties.

Not to make things worse means first and foremost to get military and dual-use exports under control. Legal and illegal exports originating in Europe have contributed to the frantic arms race in the Middle East. No attempt to dampen this race through arms control will hold unless regional powers trust that exporters, including Europe, do not contribute to clandestine arms buildups in breach of treaties and agreements. Europe has much work to do before and after the completion of the single market to prevent such exports from slipping through the weak links of the export control system within the Community. Recent activities by the Commission and within the European Political Cooperation process suggest that the Twelve have recognized the problem and are working actively on it.

As regards services, the United States is somewhat tainted in the Arab world as being biased in favor of Israel. Europe—and, of course, the former Soviet Union—are seen by Arabs as being more evenhanded and somewhat less trusted by the Israeli government. Third-party participants in inspectorates for conventional and other arms control agreements could help settle disputes during inspections on the spot and thus prevent the erosion of agreements. Europeans could positively contribute to such an inspectorate. They could also render services for overflight observations, data processing, and other equipment. Should they ever manage to set up a joint military intelligence and surveillance satellite system of their own, this would also open the possibility of offering surveillance services to the Middle East countries.

As for applying leverage, European determination to join others—the United States, the former Soviet Union—in reacting promptly and strongly to attempts to obstruct an arms control process in the region is important. As arms supplier, source of finance and technology transfer, and large market, the countries of the European Community possess more leverage than meets the eye to encourage the participants in Middle East arms control negotiations to behave constructively and cooperatively, to stick to agreements, and to abide by obligations. In the past, European diplomacy has not always given the impression that such collective determination could be achieved. As a consequence of the experiences of both the Gulf War and the Yugoslavian crisis, the future may witness a more united and effective European diplomacy.

PART IV
CONCLUSION

16

The Prospects
for Arab-Israeli Peace

STEVEN L. SPIEGEL
DAVID J. PERVIN

The search for peace between Arabs and Israelis has a long history marked by occasional successes and many failures. Active involvement by third parties has been seen as a necessary condition for fruitful negotiations, from the attempts of Count Bernadotte in the 1940s, which resulted in armistice agreements, to those of Henry Kissinger and Jimmy Carter in the 1970s, which led to disengagement agreements and then the first peace treaty between an Arab state and Israel. Indeed, given past successes, the active involvement of the United States may be seen as crucial.

The failures have been all the more spectacular, marked by the outbreak of war in 1948, 1956, 1967, 1969–1970, 1973, and 1982. Here too the role of third parties has been important. The supply of military, economic, and political support facilitated the continuation and escalation of an ultimately fruitless process of hostilities between Arabs and Israelis. At different times and for various reasons, both the United States and the USSR pursued policies that exacerbated the preexisting regional conflict.

The roles external actors play in the Arab-Israeli conflict are thus complex, all the more so because the regional actors have their own interests and do not readily accept diktats from outside. The policies and actions of the superpowers frequently had unintended outcomes—both positive, as when the Soviet-U.S. joint statement of 1977 unintentionally led Anwar Sadat to offer to visit Jerusalem, and negative, as when the prospects of Soviet-U.S. cooperation in 1969 led Gamal Abdel-Nasser to initiate the War of Attrition along the Suez Canal. While the world may have been bipolar, the actions of Middle Eastern states demonstrated that the superpowers, whether in concert or alone, could not impose their will on other actors. If there is no other lesson from the past, one that may need constant reinforcement is that the superpowers could only influence, but not determine, the course of events in the Middle East.

While the bipolar superpower competition limited the effectiveness of policies pursued by either the United States or the USSR, it should not be expected that the demise of the Soviet Union leaves the field open to U.S. hegemony, much less imperium. The debate among analysts and pundits as to the shape of the evolving international system seems somewhat academic when one considers the perspective of Middle Eastern leaderships, which is that the Americans are the only game in town. Ironically, this may make the U.S. position all the more difficult: standing alone, the United States as mediator becomes the target for complaints from one side or the other, or both, and U.S. policies are seen as favoring or compromising either the Arabs or Israel. Anwar Sadat once said that the United States holds 99 percent of the cards in the Middle East. U.S. dominance might appear even greater today than it was in the late 1970s. Even if we suppose that the odds are so heavily stacked in favor of Washington's influence, playing a winning hand still necessitates adroit diplomacy and a bit of luck. U.S. officials must confront regional parties tempted to play for a draw and hope that the United States will grow tired of the Middle Eastern game and in fatigue turn to its own concerns.

Whether the U.S. government will become tired of the game is an open question. Even before Iraq's invasion of Kuwait, the Bush administration was intensely engaged in trying to generate a peace process between Israel and the Arabs, and the Gulf War reinforced such efforts. The unprecedented prestige of the United States in the wake of the Gulf War raised hopes of a quick settlement. As a coin of the realm, prestige has limited value and even less fungibility, which became apparent in the procedural haggling between Arab and Israeli negotiators that characterized the initial bilateral negotiations during 1991 and 1992. The achievements should not be denigrated, but the hopes and expectations should be tempered. The haggling demonstrated that U.S. influence is limited and can only be employed once the regional parties genuinely seek a settlement.

As several of the contributors to this book note, however, there are questions concerning the willingness and desire of the regional parties to reach accommodation. What I. William Zartman calls a "hurting stalemate" clearly harms different parties to a greater or lesser degree. In addition, relative power positions reflect the willingness of each party to compromise on even apparently inconsequential procedural matters. It is thus no accident that the Palestinians, as Ziad Abu-Amr demonstrates, have been the most willing to forgo previously "unconditional" positions. This is because the stalemate hurts them most, they are the weakest party, and they have the most to gain from the peace process. The perceived costs of the status quo and the perceived benefits of the peace process are far less clear for the other parties.

One of the major concerns of many of the contributors has been to explore how external powers can affect the cost-benefit calculus of the regional parties. External powers have few ways of increasing the cost of intransigence, with the exception of increasing the costs by imposing sanctions on recalcitrant parties, which is unlikely. Thus, the principal instrument available to external powers to affect this calculus is through making clear both the direct and indirect, i.e., opportunity, costs of a continued stalemate. More concretely, by offering economic inducements conditional on movement toward peace, external actors can increase the benefits of a settlement and thus the opportunity costs of the status quo. The linkage imposed by the Bush administration between loan guarantees and Israeli settlement policy is one example of this strategy. This case reminds us that while the adroit use of carrots and sticks may assist in creating an environment conducive to peace, attempts to manipulate the regional parties are delicate and can easily become counterproductive. Yet, it should be remembered that the promise of extensive U.S. aid played an important role in the Egyptian-Israeli peace treaty.

Whether or not the United States will be willing or able to provide such aid is increasingly in question. Foreign aid has never been popular with the American public, and it has become less so with the lingering recession and the disappearance of the Soviet threat, which was used to justify economic and military assistance in the past. The American public is increasingly looking inward. An opportunity for other players, whether Asian or European, to step in by complementing U.S. aid may exist. It is highly unlikely that they will take it, however, given the political and economic problems and needs of Eastern Europe and Asia. Nor are the oil-rich Gulf states, still reeling from the Gulf War, likely to become major benefactors because of their large deficits. Instead of trying to underwrite peace, the Gulf states appear to be moving in the direction of increased security expenditures for themselves.

The inability or unwillingness of governments to play an active role may provide greater space for private initiatives. I. William Zartman calls for efforts by the U.S. Jewish, Arab, and Christian communities. Examples of such activities include the meetings between influential Jewish Americans and PLO Chairman Yasser Arafat in 1988 and the unprecedented trip by an American Jewish Congress delegation to Saudi Arabia in early 1992. John Marks argues that the active interaction and involvement of academics, analysts, and other interested parties could play a positive role. In recent years, many universities and independent institutions have organized meetings, conferences, and internships, bringing together participants from the Middle East with the goal of mutual education and familiarization. For example, in October 1991 the Institute on Global Cooperation and Conflict (IGCC) of the University of California sponsored a conference in Moscow that brought together prominent analysts, many with governmental connections, from the United States, Russia, Canada, Europe, and the Middle East. Many of the participants found the opportunity to meet with experts actively involved in other countries to be productive, and many reported back to their home governments. The development of informal, or in Marks's term, "shadow," interest groups with vested concerns in the continuation of the process may assist the official negotiations through offering new ideas and alternative venues for testing ideas. Indeed, the ideas offered by the contributors to this book are a prime example of the role of nonofficial parties.

While private efforts may prove helpful, it is ultimately the responsibility of government officials to make agreements. Our discussion has focused on how actors external to the Middle East can affect the regional environment in favorable ways. To the extent that they can determine the structure and process of negotiations, they will have a major impact on their outcome. Successful negotiations may be facilitated through efforts to generate an informal and convivial atmosphere in which the negotiators can become more relaxed and identify the other side not merely as an adversary but also in human terms. The famous 1982 "walk in the woods" between the top U.S. and Soviet negotiators at the INF negotiations in Geneva may serve as an example of an atmosphere facilitating success, notwithstanding the subsequent repudiation of their proposals by the two governments. At the IGCC conference in Moscow, the experience of working in small groups and even of eating together helped create an environment in which engaging in polemics and scoring debater's points was successfully discouraged.

The search for peace continues. Whether the prospects have improved is an open question, as many of the contributors to this book point out. The prospects will be enhanced only with concerted efforts by governments, specialists, and informed elites, both within and outside the Middle East. This book constitutes a contribution by experts who concentrate on the dynamics of a turbulent Middle East. The concerns they raise remain pertinent; the proposals they offer have the potential of playing a positive role in the Arab-Israeli search for peace.

The Contributors

ZIAD ABU-AMR is professor of political science at Bir Zeit University in the West Bank. He has participated in numerous conferences, seminars, and working groups focusing on the Arab-Israeli conflict. He has been a visiting scholar at the Center of Contemporary Arab Studies at Georgetown University.

JAWAD ANANI is secretary-general of the Higher Council for Science and Technology and chairman of the Jordan Technology Group. He has served as a member of the Higher Education Council of Jordan. He is author of *Reserve Pooling of Arab Common Market Countries* and *Science and Technology and Jordan's Economic Growth.*

ABDEL MONEM SAID ALY is deputy director for research and publication at the Al-Ahram Center for Political and Strategic Studies in Cairo. In Arabic, he has published books and articles on Arab relations within the regional and global orders, European integration,a nd the Arab-Israeli conflict. In English, he has published articles and chapters in the United States, France, and Sweden on Egypt's political system, national security, and arms control policies.

PATRICK CLAWSON is a resident scholar and director of the Middle East Council at the Foreign Policy Institute and editor of *Orbis.* A former senior economist at the World Bank, he is a consultant to the International Monetary Fund, the World Bank, and various U.S. government agencies on the economies of Middle Eastern and African countries. He has published numerous op-ed articles in the *New York Times, Wall Street Journal,* and *Washington Post,* among others, and coauthored with Howard

Rosen *Economic Consequences of Peace for Israel, the Palestinians, and Jordan.*

M. Z. DIAB is a Syrian strategic analyst and researcher at the Department of War Studies, King's College, London. He is also a political analyst for BBC Radio and Television and for the Gulf Centre for Strategic Studies in London. He previously served with the Syrian Ministry of Foreign Affairs and as a strategic analyst at the Syrian National Security Bureau in Damascus. His publications include chapters on U.S. and Soviet policies toward the Arab-Israeli conflict and Israel's nuclear program in *Yearbooks on Palestine: 1970, 1971, 1972* (Arabic), of which he was an assistant editor.

GIDEON FISHELSON is dean of students at Tel Aviv University and the scientific coordinator of the Armand Hammer Fund for Research on Economic Cooperation in the Middle East. He serves on various governmental committees in Israel. Among his publications is *Economic Cooperation and Middle East Peace*, edited with H. Ben-Shahar and S. Hirsh.

SHLOMO GAZIT is a senior researcher at the Jaffee Center for Strategic Studies, Tel Aviv University. After the Yom Kippur War he served as director of military intelligence of the IDF. He has served as president of Ben-Gurion University and director-general of the Jewish Agency. Among his many writings on military and Middle Eastern affairs is *The Stick and the Carrot* (Hebrew), about Israel's policy in Judea and Samaria. He edited the 1988–1989 edition of *The Middle East Military Balance.*

GALIA GOLAN is the Jay and Leonie Darwin professor of Soviet and East European Studies and director of the Mayrock Center for Soviet and East European Research at the Hebrew University of Jerusalem. She recently completed a short study on Soviet regional security proposals for the Middle East at the Woodrow Wilson Center in Washington, D.C. She is the author of numerous articles and books, including *Soviet Policies in the Middle East Since World War Two*; *The Soviet Union and the Palestine Liberation Organization: An Uneasy Alliance*; and *Yom Kippur and After: The Soviet Union and the Middle East Crisis.*

MARK A. HELLER is a senior research associate at the Jaffee Center for Strategic Studies, Tel Aviv University. He has been a visiting scholar at the Center for International Affairs, Harvard University; visiting associate professor at Cornell University; and is visiting senior fellow and coordinator of research at the Canadian Institute for International Peace and Security. His many writings on the Middle East include *No Trumpets, No Drums: A Two-State Settlement of the Israeli-Palestinian Conflict*, with Sari

Nusseibeh; *A Palestinian State: The Implications for Israel*; and "Coping With Missile Proliferation in the Middle East" (*Orbis*, Winter 1991). He edited and coauthored *The Middle East Military Balance* from 1983 to 1985 and coedited *The Soviet-American Competition in the Middle East*, with Steven L. Spiegel and Jacob Goldberg.

JOHN MARKS is president of Search for Common Ground and Common Ground Productions. He has been a U.S. foreign service officer and executive assistant to Senator Clifford Case (R-NJ). His publications include *The CIA and the Cult of Intelligence*, with Victor Marchetti, and *The Search for the "Manchurian Candidate."* In 1988 he cowrote and co-hosted, with Jonathan Kwitney, a television program entitled "What's the Common Ground Between American Arabs and Jews on the Middle East?"

HARALD MÜLLER is director of International Programs at Peace Research Institute Frankfurt. At PRIF, he dircts a multinational project on European nonproliferaton policy. Dr. Muller also teaches as visiting professor at Johns Hopkins Uniterity Center for International Relations, Bologna, and has been a member of the core group of the Program for Promoting Nuclear Nonproliferation. He has published on nuclear proliferation, European securtiy, international environmental policy, and theories of conflict and cooperation.

DAVID J. PERVIN is a graduate student in the Department of Political Science, University of California, Los Angeles. With Steven L. Spiegel he is the author of "United States Foreign Policy in the Middle East, 1989" in *Middle East Contemporary Survey*.

ALAN PLATT serves as a consultant on international and security affairs and is a visiting lecturer at Georgetown University. He previously served as chief of the Arms Transfer Division of the U.S. Arms Control and Disarmament Agency and as a senior staff member of The RAND Corporation. Among his writings are *Arms Control in the Middle East* and "European Arms Transfers to the Middle East" in *The Soviet-American Competition in the Middle East*, edited by Steven Spiegel, Mark Heller, and Jacob Goldberg.

STEVEN L. SPIEGEL is professor of political science at the University of California, Los Angeles. He has published articles on the Middle East in *The National Interest, The New Republic, Commentary, Orbis*, and the *International Studies Quarterly*. He is the author of *The Other Arab-Israeli Conflict: The Making of America's Middle East Policy from Truman to Reagan* and *Dominance and Diversity: The International Hierarchy*, and editor of *Superpower Conflict Management in the Middle East*; *The Middle East and the Western Alliance*; and *The Soviet-American Competition in the Middle East*, with Mark Heller and Jacob Goldberg.

SHIBLEY TELHAMI is associate professor of government at Cornell University. He was a 1988–1989 international fellow at the Council on Foreign Relations. He is the author of *Power and Leadership in International Bargaining: The Path to the Camp David Accords* and numerous articles on international relations and Middle East politics.

I. WILLIAM ZARTMAN is Jacob Blaustein Professor of International Organization and Conflict and director of the African Studies and Conflict Management Programs at the Paul H. Nitze School of Advanced International Studies, the Johns Hopkins University. He is a member of the Council on Foreign Relations. The author of numerous articles and books, he has written books on negotiations including *The 50% Solution*; *The Practical Negotiator*; *Ripe for Resolution*; and *International Mediation in Theory and Practice*.

Index

About the Book

With the inauguration of a new government in Israel new possibilities have emerged for a peace settlement between Arabs and Israelis. Little has been written, however, about what types of agreements the two sides might reach in such areas as arms control and economic cooperation, and because the prospects for peace have seemed so slim, there has been little discussion of the process by which the two parties might continue negotiations once they were initiated.

Responding to this lacuna, a unique group of Arab, Israeli, U.S., Canadian, and European scholars contribute to this path-breaking volume. The authors move beyond the platitudes and presumptions of peacemaking in the Middle East to address the fundamental problems that both sides will have to confront as peace becomes a realistic goal.